THE PEAK BAGGING LOG BOOK

County Tops of the United Kingdom

THE PEAK BAGGING LOG BOOK
County Tops of the United Kingdom

Copyright © Trail Wanderer Publications 2018

www.trailwanderer.co.uk

contact@trailwanderer.co.uk

First Printed 2018

Printed ISBN 978-1-9999509-4-1

By Matthew Arnold.

Editor - Scarlett Mansfield.

I, _____

have successfully reached the highest point of every county
within the United Kingdom of England, Scotland, Wales and
Northern Ireland.

Started _____, completed on _____.

INTRODUCTION

Are you ready to take on the challenge of conquering the highest point in all of the 108 counties nationwide?

Since the middle ages the ninety-two historic counties of England, Wales, Scotland and Northern Ireland once formed the geographical reference frame of the country for over one-hundred years. For more information, please visit www.abcounties.com.

It was these historic counties that laid the foundation, developing strong individual communities with a deep-rooted history. Each bringing into existence their own identities, different cultural traits, differing architecture, dialect, food, sporting organisations, and numerous traditions.

Although many of the historic boundaries remain unchanged, over the years however, there have been widespread modification in the geographical divisions of counties to meet new political requirements and to create areas used for local government.

To provide more of a challenge, this book will focus on the modern-day counties. As such, the modern counties that make up the United Kingdom total 108. There are 48 in England, 32 in Scotland, 22 in Wales, and 6 in Northern Ireland.

THE CHALLENGE OF COMPLETING ALL COUNTY TOPS

The current county tops of the United Kingdom present a diverse range of peaks, varying in both height and difficulty. From a meagre 22 meters at High Holborn in the City of London to heights of 1,345 meters on Ben Nevis in the Scottish Highlands.

Undoubtedly, however, one of the biggest challenges you will face is the geographical spread of each hilltop and the accessibility of each one. Though it would not be impossible to do without a car, it certainly would help speed up the process as public transport is not readily available to all areas of the UK. Further, the second biggest issue you may face will be time – this is undeniably a time-consuming challenge to embark on, that, may even take years to complete.

It should be noted, however, that this is an incredible feat and a rewarding experience. Admittedly, some will leave you more breathless than others, but it is a fun way to see areas of the UK that you may otherwise neglect to visit.

WHAT THIS LOG BOOK CONTAINS

Over the following pages of this book, you will find details about each county top in the United Kingdom – that includes England, Scotland, Wales and Northern Ireland. To help you complete this monumental task, this log book contains a brief description of each hill as well as statistics about it, including height, grid-reference, county location, and the category of each hill. Further, this book allows you to keep track of where you have been as well as stats such as the date you completed it, the time taken to complete it, and the total distance walked. There is even a notes section so that you can recall things you may have seen or encountered on your walk to remind you of your experience later down the line.

PRIVATE LAND DISCLAIMER

Please note, some hill summits may fall on private land - there may not be any accessible public rights of way to reach the top. Please remember to be respectful and seek permission from the landowner before venturing onto private land.

HILL CATEGORIES

To understand the type of hill/mountain you will face, it is useful to know about the different classifications that exist across the United Kingdom.

COUNTRY HIGH POINT

The highest geographical location in a country in relation to Earth's sea level.

HISTORIC COUNTY TOP

The historic county top refers to the highest point of the traditional counties, areas that were established for administration by the Normans; they are also known as ancient counties. Though their boundaries still exist, since 1965 many changes have been made to local government and administrative areas.

MUNRO

The name Munro is given to mountains in Scotland with a height that exceeds 3,000 ft (914 m). Ben Nevis is the best-known of this range as it is also the highest mountain in the United Kingdom. According to the Scottish Mountaineering Club, in total, there are 282 Munros and 227 subsidiary tops.

MARILYN

Alan Dawson originally created the 'Marilyn' classification in his book, The Relative Hills of Britain in 1992. The name Marylin defines a peak with a prominence above 150 metres, regardless of height. Prominence, incidentally, refers to the height of the peak's summit relative to the lowest contour line that encircles it but that contains no higher summit within it.

HEWITT

In the UK, Hewitt refers to a mountain peak with a height of 2,000 ft (610 m) or greater. Alan Dawson also proposed the acronym Hewitt in his same book, The Relative Hills of Britain (1992). Hewitt, in this case, stood for Hills in England, Wales and Ireland over Two Thousand feet in height. There are 209 in Ireland, 135 in Wales, and 180 in England - totalling 524 Hewitts in all.

NUTTALL

The term Nuttall applies only to mountains in England and Wales that are over 2,000 ft (610 m). John and Anne Nuttall put forward this classification in their publication, The Mountains of England & Wales (1989). There are currently 446 Nuttalls.

HARDY

A Hardy classifies hills or mountains that are the highest point in a hill range, a UK Island over 1000 acres or a high point of an administrive area. Ian Hardy coined the term in the early 1990s and published a booklet The Hardys - The UK's High Points. There are 347 Hardys in the United Kingdom, 183 in England, 107 in Scotland, 31 in Wales and 26 in Northern Ireland.

VANDELEUR-LYNAMS

There are 273 Vandeleur-Lynams in Ireland. They are the Irish equivalent of a Nuttall. The difference being that the definition is fully metric. A height of 600 metres (1,969 ft), and a prominence of 15 metres (49 ft) is required.

WAINWRIGHT

The British fell walker, Alfred Wainwright, published seven guides known as the Pictorial Guides to the Lakeland Fells (1955-1966). In this series, Wainwright detailed the fells of the Lake District National Park. The 214 fells included in this series of books have now fallen into their own category and are named after Wainwright himself.

ENGLAND COUNTY TOPS

As of 2009, there are forty-eight ceremonial counties in England. The table is ranked in order from highest county top to smallest. ☑

1. Cumbria	☐	2. Northumberland	☐
3. Durham	☐	4. North Yorkshire	☐
5. Herefordshire	☐	6. Derbyshire	☐
7. Lancashire	☐	8. Devon	☐
9. West Yorkshire	☐	10. Cheshire	☐
11. South Yorkshire	☐	12. Greater Manchester	☐
13. Shropshire	☐	14. Staffordshire	☐
15. Somerset	☐	16. Worcestershire	☐
17. Cornwall	☐	18. Gloucestershire	☐
19. Berkshire	☐	20. Surrey	☐
21. Wiltshire	☐	22. Hampshire	☐
23. West Sussex	☐	24. Dorset	☐
25. Leicestershire	☐	26. West Midlands	☐
27. Buckinghamshire	☐	28. Oxfordshire	☐
29. Warwickshire	☐	30. Tyne and Wear	☐
31. Kent	☐	32. East Sussex	☐
33. East Riding of Yorkshire	☐	34. Greater London	☐
35. Hertfordshire	☐	36. Bedfordshire	☐
37. Isle of Wight	☐	38. Northamptonshire	☐
39. Nottinghamshire	☐	40. Rutland	☐
41. Merseyside	☐	42. Lincolnshire	☐
43. Bristol	☐	44. Essex	☐
45. Cambridgeshire	☐	46. Suffolk	☐
47. Norfolk	☐	48. City of London	☐

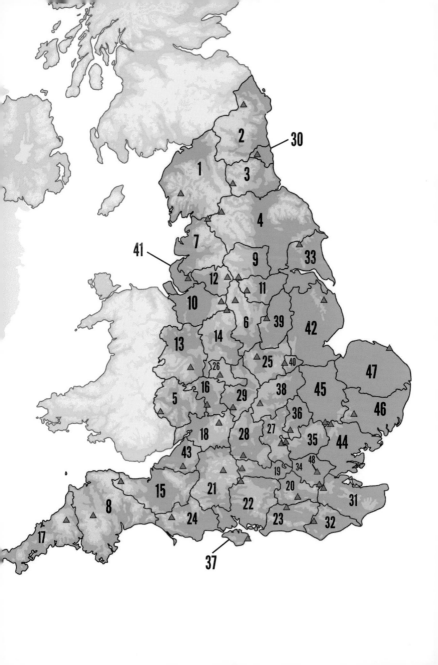

⌂ **Height:** 3,209 ft (978 m) ⊕ **County:** Cumbria

○ **Region:** Lake District ◉ **Lat/Long:** 54.454223, -3.211602

◉ **Grid Ref:** NY 215 072 ▥ **OS Map:** OL 6

▣ **Category:** Country High Point, Historic County Top, Current County Top, Marilyn, Hewitt, Wainwright, Nuttall

With an elevation of 3,209 ft (978 m), Scafell Pike is well-known for being the tallest mountain in England. Scafell Pike is located in the renowned Lake District National Park and makes up part of the Southern Fells, Cumbria. Neighbouring civil parishes of Wasdale, Borrowdale, Eskdale, and Langdale all provide excellent starting points to reach the summit.

Lord Leconfield donated the surrounding land around the peak to the National Trust in 1919 to honour all those who served in the Great War. The summit is made up of rough crags; a large cairn also holds England's highest memorial plaque. The peak is one out of the three climbed when taking part in the popular Three Peaks Challenge.

LOG

Date:	Week No:
Start Point:	Day:
Start Time:	Pace:
Finish Time:	Total Ascent:
Elapsed Time:	Total Distance:

THE CHEVIOT

⛰	**Height:**	2,674 ft (815 m)	
🌐	**County:**	Northumberland	
⬤	**Region:**	Cheviot Hills	
◉	**Lat/Long:**	55.47823, -2.14553	
⦿	**Grid Ref:**	NT 909 205	
🗺	**OS Map:**	OL 16	

🖼 **Category:** Historic County Top, Current County Top, Marilyn, Hewitt, Nuttall

The Cheviot, at 2,674 ft (815 m) high, is located in the north of England, close to the Scottish border. It is the highest point in Northumberland and the Cheviot Hills. It is also the last of the major peaks on the 286-mile Pennine Way.

The summit is mainly flat and is covered by a surrounding, far-reaching, peat bog that is up to 2 m deep in places. Stone slabs provide a safe route to reach the summit. Further to the north of the summit, the wreckage of a B-17 bomber can be found as it crashed there during World War Two.

LOG

Date:	Week No:
Start Point:	Day:
Start Time:	Pace:
Finish Time:	Total Ascent:
Elapsed Time:	Total Distance:

MICKLE FELL

△ **Height:** 2,585 ft (788 m)   ⊕ **County:** Durham

○ **Region:** Pennines   ◉ **Lat/Long:** 54.615715, -2.30186

◎ **Grid Ref:** NY 805 245   ▥ **OS Map:** OL 19

▣ **Category:** Historic County Top, Current County Top, Marilyn, Hewitt, Nuttall

With an elevation of 2,585 ft (788 m), the distinctive Mickle Fell mountain sits within a large area of boggy moorland in the Pennines. It is the highest point in County Durham. The route to the summit requires a long hike regardless of your chosen route.

The summit falls within the Warcop Training Area, one of the largest military training areas in the UK. Access days are limited to times when live firing is not taking place. If you see red flags flying, do not enter the area. More information on firing days can be found using the following link below.

(www.gov.uk/government/publications/warcop-access-times)

LOG

Date:	Week No:
Start Point:	Day:
Start Time:	Pace:
Finish Time:	Total Ascent:
Elapsed Time:	Total Distance:

WHERNSIDE

⌂ **Height:** 2,415 ft (736 m)

⊕ **County:** North Yorkshire

○ **Region:** Yorkshire Dales

◉ **Lat/Long:** 54.22764, -2.40338

◉ **Grid Ref:** SD 738 814

▥ **OS Map:** OL 2

🖻 **Category:** Historic County Top, Current County Top, Marilyn, Hewitt, Nuttall

Whernside is situated in the north of England. Located within the Yorkshire Dales, with an elevation of 2,415 ft (736 m), it is the highest of the Yorkshire's Three Peaks. The mountain forms a long ridge and views from the summit stretch over to the Lake District, Morecambe Bay, and on a clear day, even Blackpool tower, located some 40 miles away.

To follow the most straight-forward route to the summit, start at Ribblehead. This route will take you past the magnificent Victorian Ribblehead Viaduct constructed in the 1870s.

LOG

Date:	Week No:
Start Point:	Day:
Start Time:	Pace:
Finish Time:	Total Ascent:
Elapsed Time:	Total Distance:

BLACK MOUNTAIN

⌂ **Height:** 2,306 ft (703 m) ⊕ **County:** Herefordshire

○ **Region:** Black Mountains ⊙ **Lat/Long:** 52.008333, -3.084722

◉ **Grid Ref:** SO 255 350 ▥ **OS Map:** OL 13

▣ **Category:** Current County Top, Marilyn, Hewitt, Nuttall

At 2,306 ft (703 m) high , Black Mountain, also known as Twyn Llech, is the highest point within the Black Mountains in the county of Herefordshire. It is also the only Marilyn to straddle the Welsh-English border.

The summit can be reached by passing along part of Offa's Dyke, the long-distance trail that roughly follows the border between England and Wales. The summit is unmarked but falls on open access land thus allowing deviation from the path. The ground is peaty and remains very wet even in good conditions.

LOG

Date:	Week No:
Start Point:	Day:
Start Time:	Pace:
Finish Time:	Total Ascent:
Elapsed Time:	Total Distance:

KINDER SCOUT

⌂ **Height:** 2,087 ft (636 m)　⊕ **County:** Derbyshire

○ **Region:** Peak District　◉ **Lat/Long:** 53.3845, -1.87343136

◎ **Grid Ref:** SK 085 875　▥ **OS Map:** OL 1

▣ **Category:** Historic County Top, Current County Top, Marilyn, Hewitt, Nuttall

Kinder Scout stands at 2,087 ft (636 m). It is the highest point within the Peak District and the county of Derbyshire. The peak forms part of the Pennine Way and the summit is accessible from the villages of Hayfield or Edale.

Kinder Downfall, the tallest waterfall in the Peak District, is located close to the summit area. With strong wind conditions, the water blows back on itself resulting in a cloud of spray across the area.

The site was also famously part of the 1932 mass trespass of 500 walkers – an event to raise awareness of how ramblers in England and Wales were being denied access to various areas of open country. The event subsequently secured the right to explore the open country for all. (Hooray!)

LOG

Date:	Week No:
Start Point:	**Day:**
Start Time:	**Pace:**
Finish Time:	**Total Ascent:**
Elapsed Time:	**Total Distance:**

⌂ **Height:** 2,060 ft (628 m)   ⊕ **County:** Lancashire

○ **Region:** Yorkshire Dales   ◉ **Lat/Long:** 54.2085, -2.48001784

⊙ **Grid Ref:** SD 687 793   ▥ **OS Map:** OL 2

🖼 **Category:** Current County Top, Marilyn, Hewitt, Nuttall

Gargareth sits within the Yorkshire Dales. At 2,060 ft (628 m), it is the highest point in Lancashire. The mountain is littered with crags, potholes, and limestone caves that descend to form a network of passages in some places. The mountain lies to the north on Ingleton and can be reached from either Leck, Ireby, or Leck Fell House.

A trig point marks the summit; it is close to what is believed to be one of the highest dry stoned walls in the country that marks the county boundary. The summit provides fantastic views towards Morecambe Bay and over to the Lake District.

LOG

Date:		**Week No:**	
Start Point:		**Day:**	
Start Time:		**Pace:**	
Finish Time:		**Total Ascent:**	
Elapsed Time:		**Total Distance:**	

HIGH WILLHAYS

⛰️ **Height:** 2,037 ft (621 m) 🌐 **County:** Devon

⭕ **Region:** Dartmoor ◉ **Lat/Long:** 50.6851, -4.0111046

📍 **Grid Ref:** SX 580 892 📖 **OS Map:** OL 28

🖼️ **Category:** Historic County Top, Current County Top, Marilyn, Hewitt, Nuttall

Standing at 2,037 ft (621 m) tall, High Willhays is located on the north-western edge of Dartmoor National Park in Devon. It sits 3 miles south of the town of Okehampton and is the highest point in the UK (south of the Brecon Beacons). Well-maintained roads pass close to the area and there are various parking bays located nearby, from whee you can do a short but steep walk to the summit.

The peak consists of rocky outcrops, the largest of which is marked with a cairn. Please bear in mind that the hilltop does fall within a military firing range - red flags are raised around the perimeter when in use. Active firing days can be checked by visiting the following link:

(www.gov.uk/government/publications/dartmoor-firing-programme)

LOG

Date:	Week No:
Start Point:	Day:
Start Time:	Pace:
Finish Time:	Total Ascent:
Elapsed Time:	Total Distance:

BLACK HILL

⌂ **Height:** 1,909 ft (582 m)   ⊕ **County:** West Yorkshire

○ **Region:** Peak District   ◉ **Lat/Long:** 53.5388, -1.8835472

◎ **Grid Ref:** SE 078 046   ▥ **OS Map:** OL 1

▨ **Category:** Historic County Top, Current County Top, Marilyn

At 1,909 ft (582 m) tall, Black hill is located in the Peak District. Once the highest point in the historic county of Cheshire, the peak now lies on the border of West Yorkshire and Derbyshire. Instead, it is now the highest point in the county of West Yorkshire.

The appropriately named hill is peaty and becomes very boggy after heavy rain. There is no vegetation around the summit area and it makes the ground around it very dark. The summit is crossed by the Pennine Way from Crowden. A paved surface, laid by authorities, allows walkers to reach the top with relative ease.

LOG

Date:	Week No:
Start Point:	Day:
Start Time:	Pace:
Finish Time:	Total Ascent:
Elapsed Time:	Total Distance:

SHINING TOR

⌂ **Height:** 1,834 ft (559 m) ⊕ **County:** Cheshire

○ **Region:** Peak District ⊚ **Lat/Long:** 53.2608, -2.00946439

⊙ **Grid Ref:** SJ 994 737 ▥ **OS Map:** OL 24

🖼 **Category:** Current County Top, Marilyn

Shining Tor, at 1,834 ft (559 m) high, lies on the border of Derbyshire and Cheshire and is the tallest peak in Cheshire. The hill is situated within the Peak District, located between the towns of Buxton and Macclesfield.

The summit is accessible using several different paths. The most popular of which starts at the Goyt Valley near to Errwood Reservoir. Looking out over the Cheshire plain from the summit, in good conditions, you will be able to spot many notable landmarks including Winter Hill, Manchester, and even Snowdonia in exceptionally good conditions.

LOG

Date:	Week No:
Start Point:	Day:
Start Time:	Pace:
Finish Time:	Total Ascent:
Elapsed Time:	Total Distance:

HIGH STONES

⛰ **Height:** 1,798 ft (548 m)   🌐 **County:** South Yorkshire

⭕ **Region:** Peak District   ◉ **Lat/Long:** 53.44514, -1.71842

📍 **Grid Ref:** SK 188 943   🗺 **OS Map:** OL 1

🖼 **Category:** Current County Top

High Stones, found at 1,798 ft (548 m), falls within the boundaries of Sheffield Council; it is the highest point of the county of South Yorkshire. It lies on Howden Moors, near the boundary of the Peak District, between Howden Reservoir and Langsett Reservoir.

The summit can be reached from Fairholmes Car Park, situated near Derwent Reservoir. The area is managed by the National Trust as part of their High Park Estate. A cairn, over two feet tall, is located at the top to mark the summit.

LOG

Date:	Week No:
Start Point:	Day:
Start Time:	Pace:
Finish Time:	Total Ascent:
Elapsed Time:	Total Distance:

BLACK CHEW HEAD

⌂ **Height:** 1,778 ft (542 m) ⊕ **County:** Greater Manchester

○ **Region:** Peak District ◉ **Lat/Long:** 53.5145, -1.91673378

◉ **Grid Ref:** SE 056 019 ▥ **OS Map:** OL 1

▣ **Category:** Current County Top, Marilyn

Black Chew Head stands on moorland situated at the edge of the Peak District, bordering Derbyshire. At 1,778 ft (542 m) high, it is the highest point in the metropolitan county of Greater Manchester.

The hill is accessible using several different routes. The most obvious path to the summit, where a small cairn can be found, begins at Dovestone Reservoir in Greenfield. The hill notably features numerous gritstone edges. At the peak, you can find views overlooking the Chew Valley to the east, and north to Dovestone Reservoir.

LOG

Date:	Week No:
Start Point:	Day:
Start Time:	Pace:
Finish Time:	Total Ascent:
Elapsed Time:	Total Distance:

BROWN CLEE HILL 13

⌂ **Height:** 1,772 ft (540 m)   ⊕ **County:** Shropshire

○ **Region:** Shropshire Hills   ◉ **Lat/Long:** 52.4668, -2.60111074

⦿ **Grid Ref:** SO 593 865   ▥ **OS Map:** OS 217

🖾 **Category:** Historic County Top, Current County Top, Marilyn

Brown Clee Hill, at 1,772 ft (540 m) tall, is the highest point in Shropshire. It is located in the Shropshire Hills, an Area of Outstanding Natural Beauty. The hill is made up of two peaks Abdon Burf and Clee Burf, with the highest being Abdon Burf. Much of the hill is private land: the eastern side is owned by Viscount Boyne while much of the western fringes by private landowners. Large coniferous plants cover the slopes.

During World War Two, this hill was the site of numerous aircraft accidents for both allied and German forces. The summit hosts a microwave relay station. A toposcope can be found at the top too and highlights various, notable landmarks nearby.

LOG

Date:	Week No:
Start Point:	Day:
Start Time:	Pace:
Finish Time:	Total Ascent:
Elapsed Time:	Total Distance:

CHEEKS HILL

⛰ **Height:** 1,706 ft (520 m)   🌐 **County:** Staffordshire

⭕ **Region:** Peak District   ◎ **Lat/Long:** 53.2269, -1.96151102

◉ **Grid Ref:** SK 026 699   🗺 **OS Map:** OL 24

🖼 **Category:** Historic County Top, Current County Top, Marilyn

Cheeks Hill stands at 1,706 ft (520 m); it is the highest point in the county of Staffordshire. The hill lies on Axe Edge Moor, a substantial area of moorland located southwest of Buxton in the Peak District. It constitutes some of the most rugged countryside to be found in the Midlands.

The walk to the top can be made from the village of Flash. In good visibility, the summit provides striking views over the Cheshire plain and as far as The Wrekin hill in East Shropshire. Close to the summit, a dry-stone wall can be found marking the Staffordshire – Derbyshire border.

LOG

Date:	Week No:
Start Point:	Day:
Start Time:	Pace:
Finish Time:	Total Ascent:
Elapsed Time:	Total Distance:

DUNKERY BEACON

⛰ **Height:** 1,703 ft (519 m) 🌐 **County:** Somerset

⭕ **Region:** Exmoor ◎ **Lat/Long:** 51.1674, -3.58172332

📍 **Grid Ref:** SS 891 415 🗺 **OS Map:** OL 9

🖼 **Category:** Historic County Top, Current County Top, Marilyn

Dunkery Beacon sits within Exmoor National Park. At 1,703 ft (519 m), it is the second highest point in southern England, outside of Dartmoor. The hill is located on an area of special importance as humans have visited the site since the Bronze Age. You can find several burial mounds in the form of cairns and bowl barrows in the surrounding area of the summit.

The hill was under private ownership until Thomas Acland donated it to the National Trust in 1935. The shortest route to reach the large cairn on the summit is via the car park located at Dunkery Gate. Views stretch across Devon, Somerset, and even across to Wales on a good day.

LOG

Date:		**Week No:**	
Start Point:		**Day:**	
Start Time:		**Pace:**	
Finish Time:		**Total Ascent:**	
Elapsed Time:		**Total Distance:**	

⛰ **Height:** 1,394 ft (425 m) ⊕ **County:** Worcestershire

○ **Region:** Malvern Hills ◉ **Lat/Long:** 52.1048, -2.33910191

◉ **Grid Ref:** SO 768 452 ▥ **OS Map:** OS 190

🖼 **Category:** Historic County Top, Current County Top, Marilyn

Worcestershire beacon, more popularly known as Worcester Beacon, has an elevation of 1,394 ft (425 m) and is the highest point of the Malvern Hills. The Malvern Hills are a group of hills that span the counties of Worcestershire, Herefordshire, and a small area of Gloucestershire. The hills are managed by the Malvern Hills Conservators who preserve the landscape.

In 1588 the area was used as a site to place a signalling beacon. It formed part of a chain of warning beacons to alert people when the Spanish Armada attempted to invade England. It is popular with walkers and the summit can be reached via its vast network of footpaths. A toposcope can also be found at the top. Officials erected the device in 1897 to commemorate Queen Victoria's Diamond Jubilee.

LOG

Date:	Week No:
Start Point:	Day:
Start Time:	Pace:
Finish Time:	Total Ascent:
Elapsed Time:	Total Distance:

⌂	**Height:**	1,378 ft (420 m)	**County:**	Cornwall
○	**Region:**	Bodmin Moor	**Lat/Long:**	50.5906, -4.6027286
⦿	**Grid Ref:**	SX 158 800	**OS Map:**	OS 109
🖼	**Category:**	Historic County Top, Current County Top, Marilyn		

Brown Willy is a hill steeped in history, located on Bodmin Moor, a granite moorland where many of Cornwall's rivers begin. At 1,378 ft (420 m) in elevation, it is the highest hill in the county of Cornwall.

Upon reaching the summit, a trig point can be found located next to a cairn. The cairns located nearby are believed to date back to the early Bronze Age; it has been considered a sacred place for centuries. The cairns have never been excavated and folklore speculates that an ancient Cornish King may even be buried underneath one of them.

LOG

Date:	**Week No:**
Start Point:	**Day:**
Start Time:	**Pace:**
Finish Time:	**Total Ascent:**
Elapsed Time:	**Total Distance:**

CLEEVE HILL

⌂ **Height:** 1,083 ft (330 m)   ⊕ **County:** Gloucestershire

○ **Region:** Cleeve Common   ◉ **Lat/Long:** 51.9198, -2.00586148

⦾ **Grid Ref:** SO 996 245   ▥ **OS Map:** OS 179

▤ **Category:** Historic County Top, Current County Top, Marilyn

Cleeve Hill, with a height of 1,083 ft (330 m), is the highest point in Gloucestershire. It is located in the Cotswolds amongst Cleeve Common, a designated Area of Outstanding Natural Beauty and a site of Special Scientific Interest. Belas Knap, a Neolithic chambered tomb, exists close to the summit along with an Iron Age hillfort on its western slopes.

A golf course has also existed on the hill since 1891. A nearby car park provides a short walk to the summit. A trig point and toposcope are located at the top. The views extend over Cheltenham racecourse and over into Wales. On a very clear day, with good visibility, the view can extend 90 miles to Winsford Hill on Exmoor.

LOG

Date:	Week No:
Start Point:	Day:
Start Time:	Pace:
Finish Time:	Total Ascent:
Elapsed Time:	Total Distance:

WALBURY HILL

⌂ **Height:**	974 ft (297 m)	⊕ **County:**	Berkshire
○ **Region:**	North Wessex Downs	⊙ **Lat/Long:**	51.3525, -1.46507073
⊙ **Grid Ref:**	SU 373 616	⊞ **OS Map:**	OS 158
▣ **Category:**	Historic County Top, Current County Top, Marilyn		

Walbury Hill, at 974 ft (297 m), is the highest point in the wild grasslands of the North Wessex Downs, Berkshire. The hill sits in the southwest corner of Berkshire and extends as a ridge into nearby Hampshire and Wiltshire. It is a popular spot for paragliders.

Before the use of satellites, the BBC used the hill as a relay station during the Newbury Races. A car park can be found either side of the hill, a short walk from the summit. The summit itself is marked by a trig point, near to where the long-distance footpath the Test Way proceeds. This hill is also the start point of the Wayfarers Walk.

LOG

Date:	**Week No:**
Start Point:	**Day:**
Start Time:	**Pace:**
Finish Time:	**Total Ascent:**
Elapsed Time:	**Total Distance:**

LEITH HILL

⛰ **Height:** 968 ft (295 m)   🌐 **County:** Surrey

⭕ **Region:** Surrey Hills   ◉ **Lat/Long:** 51.1765, -0.37149073

📍 **Grid Ref:** TQ 139 431   🗺 **OS Map:** OS 146

🖼 **Category:** Historic County Top, Current County Top, Marilyn, Hardy

Leith Hill stands at a modest height of 968 ft (295 m). It is a wooded hill located in the Surrey Hills, an Area of Outstanding Natural Beauty. It is also the highest point in the county of Surrey.

The hill played a historic role as it is believed to have been the location of a battle between the Saxons and Danes in the ninth century. Ethelwulf, the father of Alfred the Great, took up position on the slopes to win the battle to stop the Danes from further conquests.

Leith Hill Tower, owned by the National Trust, is situated at the summit. Richard Hull built the tower in 1767; there are 74 steps up the spiral staircase to the top and views stretch as far as the Wembley Stadium Arch and the London Eye.

LOG

Date:	Week No:
Start Point:	Day:
Start Time:	Pace:
Finish Time:	Total Ascent:
Elapsed Time:	Total Distance:

⌂ **Height:** 965 ft (294 m)   ⊕ **County:** Wiltshire

○ **Region:** North Wessex Downs   ⊕ **Lat/Long:** 51.3778, -1.85160131

⊙ **Grid Ref:** SU 104 643   ▥ **OS Map:** OS 157

▣ **Category:** Historic County Top, Current County Top, Hardy

Milk Hill, at 965 ft (294 m) tall, is the second highest chalk hill in the UK and the highest point in the county of Wiltshire. It is also the highest summit of a ridge that runs 50 km from the South Downs, across the Chilterns into Wiltshire. A route to the summit can be made from the car park located on a minor road between Lockeridge and Alton Barnes.

Located nearby is Alton Barnes White horse, a chalk hill figure approximately 180 feet high and 160 feet long, cut in 1812. Views from the summit extend as far as the Mendips and Cotswolds. In good conditions, the Black Mountains in Wales can also be seen.

LOG

Date:	Week No:
Start Point:	Day:
Start Time:	Pace:
Finish Time:	Total Ascent:
Elapsed Time:	Total Distance:

PILOT HILL

⏶ **Height:** 938 ft (286 m)   ⊕ **County:** Hampshire

○ **Region:** North Wessex Downs   ⊕ **Lat/Long:** 51.3387, -1.42899426

⊙ **Grid Ref:** SU 398 601   ▥ **OS Map:** OS 158

🖼 **Category:** Historic County Top, Current County Top

At 938 ft (286 m), Pilot Hill is the highest point in the county of Hampshire. The hill lies 7 miles southwest of Newbury, close to the border of Hampshire and Berkshire. The hill is part of the north-facing escarpment on the North Hampshire Downs, a large area of downland that extends from the South Downs to the Dorset Downs.

The summit can be reached by passing along the Brenda Parker Way, a 78-mile long-distance footpath running from Aldershot to Andover. The upper slopes are open grassland while the lower slopes are covered in woodland. The north face of the hill lies within West Berkshire.

LOG

Date:	Week No:
Start Point:	Day:
Start Time:	Pace:
Finish Time:	Total Ascent:
Elapsed Time:	Total Distance:

BLACK DOWN

⌂ **Height:** 919 ft (280 m)   ⊕ **County:** West Sussex

○ **Region:** South Downs   ◉ **Lat/Long:** 51.0584, -0.68985872

⊚ **Grid Ref:** SU 919 296   ▭ **OS Map:** OL 33

▣ **Category:** Historic County Top, Current County Top, Marilyn

Black Down stands at a height of 919 ft (280 m) and is the highest point in the county of West Sussex. It is also the highest point in the South Downs National Park. The hill has a strong literary connection with the Victorian poet Alfred Tennyson and is currently owned by the National Trust. When it comes to terrain, the area is covered in pine and heather. A route to the summit can be made from a small car park off Fernden Lane, located to the southeast of the hill.

In November 1967, tragedy struck in the area. An aeroplane, flying from Malaga to Heathrow and owned by the Spanish airline Iberian Airlines, crashed close by. All 37 passengers on board died – including June Thorburn, a popular English Actress at the time.

LOG

Date:	Week No:
Start Point:	Day:
Start Time:	Pace:
Finish Time:	Total Ascent:
Elapsed Time:	Total Distance:

LEWESDON HILL

⛰ **Height:** 915 ft (279 m)   🌐 **County:** Dorset

⭕ **Region:** Dorset AONB   ◈ **Lat/Long:** 50.8073, -2.79933489

📍 **Grid Ref:** ST 437 011   🗺 **OS Map:** OS 116

🖼 **Category:** Historic County Top, Current County Top, Marilyn, Hardy

Standing at 915 ft (279 m), the elongated ridge of Lewesdon Hill is the highest point in the county of Dorset. The summit is surrounded by beech woods and can be found at the east end of the ridge. There are two main footpaths leading up to the summit: one from the village of Broadwindsor and the other from Coombe Lane. Views stretch over Devon, Somerset, and out to sea.

Like so many of the hills in Dorset, an Iron Age hillfort once stood on the top. The original bank and ditches are still visible. Later, it was used as an Armada Beacon to warn of the impending Spanish attack in 1558.

LOG

Date:	Week No:
Start Point:	Day:
Start Time:	Pace:
Finish Time:	Total Ascent:
Elapsed Time:	Total Distance:

⛰ **Height:** 912 ft (278 m) 🌐 **County:** Leicestershire

⭘ **Region:** The National Forest 📍 **Lat/Long:** 52.7145, -1.32070438

📍 **Grid Ref:** SK 459 131 📖 **OS Map:** OS 245

🖼 **Category:** Historic County Top, Current County Top, Marilyn

Bardon Hill, at 912 ft (278 m), is the highest point in the county of Leicestershire. It is located in 'The National Forest' and was once a former volcano. It sits directly upon an old fault line known as Thringstone Fault; it starts in Derbyshire and stretches across to Germany.

The summit sits at the eastern-edge of Bardon Hill Quarry, an operational site dating back 400 years. The top of the hill hosts both a trig point and radio mast. On a clear day with good visibility, you can see as far as the Malvern and Shropshire Hills, and even the Lincoln Cathedral, nearly 50 miles away.

LOG

Date:	Week No:
Start Point:	Day:
Start Time:	Pace:
Finish Time:	Total Ascent:
Elapsed Time:	Total Distance:

TURNERS HILL

⌂	**Height:** 883 ft (269 m)	⊕ **County:** West Midlands	
○	**Region:** Rowley Hills	◉ **Lat/Long:** 52.5227, -2.13483743	
◎	**Grid Ref:** SO 967 887	▥ **OS Map:** OS 219	
▨	**Category:** Current County Top		

Turners Hill has an elevation of 883 ft (269 m). It is the highest hill in the West Midlands and forms part of the Rowley Hills. It is situated to the north of Rowley Regis, next to a quarry. Dudley Golf Club is also located next to the hilltop.

To reach the summit, walkers simply have to make the short journey from the nearby road, Portway Hill. At the top of the hill, you can find two large radio transmission towers. Views stretch across to Clent Hills, Shatterford Hill, Birmingham, and the Black Country. With good visibility, you can see as far as Shropshire and the Malvern Hills.

LOG

Date:	Week No:
Start Point:	Day:
Start Time:	Pace:
Finish Time:	Total Ascent:
Elapsed Time:	Total Distance:

HADDINGTON HILL

⌂ **Height:** 876 ft (267 m)

⊕ **County:** Buckinghamshire

○ **Region:** Chilterns

◉ **Lat/Long:** 51.7723, -0.71079254

⊙ **Grid Ref:** SP 890 090

▥ **OS Map:** OS 181

▨ **Category:** Historic County Top, Current County Top, Marilyn

Haddington Hill is the highest point in the county of Buckinghamshire. The summit sits 876 ft (267 m) above sea level and is located in the Chilterns, a chalk escarpment covering an area of 833 km^2. The hill is owned by the Forestry Commission - Wendover Woods covers over 800 acres.

There are many trails that can be found among the forest and that are accessible by car. A car park can be found located nearby. Since the summit is flat, the top of Haddington Hill is hard to determine. In the woods, east of the carpark, you will find a series of large stones bearing the inscription "The Chiltern Summit".

LOG

Date:	Week No:
Start Point:	Day:
Start Time:	Pace:
Finish Time:	Total Ascent:
Elapsed Time:	Total Distance:

WHITEHORSE HILL

⛰ **Height:** 856 ft (261 m)　⊕ **County:** Oxfordshire

○ **Region:** North Wessex Downs　⊕ **Lat/Long:** 51.5755, -1.56729888

◎ **Grid Ref:** SU 300 863　🗺 **OS Map:** OS170

🖼 **Category:** Current County Top

Whitehorse Hill, with an elevation of 856 ft (261 m), is a very unique place. It is the location of a highly-stylised, prehistoric hill figure, featuring a 110 m long white horse formed from deep trenches filled with crushed white chalk. The hill forms part of a range of chalk downland hills. The horse is believed to date back to the Iron Age.

The summit is a short walk from the White Horse car park. Nearby, you can also find Uffington Castle, an early Iron Age hillfort. The site is owned and managed by the National Trust.

LOG

Date:	Week No:
Start Point:	Day:
Start Time:	Pace:
Finish Time:	Total Ascent:
Elapsed Time:	Total Distance:

EBRINGTON HILL

⛰ **Height:** 856 ft (261 m)   🌐 **County:** Warwickshire

⭕ **Region:** Cotswolds   ◈ **Lat/Long:** 52.0814, -1.72819224

📍 **Grid Ref:** SP 187 426   📖 **OS Map:** OL 45

🖼 **Category:** Historic County Top, Current County Top

At 856 ft (261 m), Ebrington Hill is the highest point in the county of Warwickshire. It is located east of the village of Ilmington and west of the village of Mickleton.

Sitting on the border of the Cotswolds, the hilltop is accessible from a road that runs directly next to the summit. A trig point can be found at the top, a short distance behind the radio transmission towers and building. The Monarch's Way, a long-distance footpath, passes through the nearby village of Hidcote Bartrim.

LOG

Date:	Week No:
Start Point:	Day:
Start Time:	Pace:
Finish Time:	Total Ascent:
Elapsed Time:	Total Distance:

CURROCK HILL

- ⏶ **Height:** 850 ft (259 m)
- ⊕ **County:** Tyne and Wear
- ○ **Region:** Gateshead
- ⊙ **Lat/Long:** 54.9274, -1.83424024
- ⊙ **Grid Ref:** NZ 107 592
- ▥ **OS Map:** OS 307
- 🖼 **Category:** Current County Top

Currock Hill sits at 850 ft (259 m). It is the highest point in the county of Tyne and Wear and the metropolitan borough of Gateshead. Its name is derived from the Celtic word 'currock', a word for cairn or stack of stones.

The hilltop sits northwest of the village Chopwell and forms part of the watershed divide between the catchments of the River Tyne and River Derwent. The hill offers panoramic views towards the Pennines, Tyne Valley, Cheviot Hills, and the North Sea coast.

There has also been a long-standing association with flying around Currock Hill. During World War One, the hill acted as an airfield for 36 Squadron of the Royal Flying Corp.

LOG

Date:	Week No:
Start Point:	Day:
Start Time:	Pace:
Finish Time:	Total Ascent:
Elapsed Time:	Total Distance:

BETSOM'S HILL

⛰ **Height:** 823 ft (251 m)

🌐 **County:** Kent

◯ **Region:** Kent Downs

◎ **Lat/Long:** 51.2888, 0.05373296

◎ **Grid Ref:** TQ 435 563

🗺 **OS Map:** OS 147

🖼 **Category:** Historic County Top, Current County Top

Betsom's Hill stands at 823 ft (251 m) high and is the highest point in the county of Kent. This hill is part of the North Downs, a ridge of chalk hills located in the south-east of Kent between Westerham and Tatsfield.

The hilltop is unmarked and access is not open to the public. It is the only county top located on private land. If you wish to visit, permission should be sought from the landowner prior to stepping foot on the land. Despite this inconvenience, the long-distance trail the North Downs Way passes below the summit of the hill.

At one point, Victorian-era citizen's built a defence fort on the crest of the hill to protect London from foreign invaders crossing the channel. It formed part of the London Defence scheme and acted as a mobilisation centre for volunteer troops as well as an ammunition store.

LOG

Date:	Week No:
Start Point:	Day:
Start Time:	Pace:
Finish Time:	Total Ascent:
Elapsed Time:	Total Distance:

DITCHLING BEACON

⌂ **Height:** 814 ft (248 m) ⊕ **County:** East Sussex

○ **Region:** South Downs ◉ **Lat/Long:** 50.902, -0.10720845

◎ **Grid Ref:** TQ 331 130 ▥ **OS Map:** OL 11

🖼 **Category:** Historic County Top, Current County Top, Marilyn

Ditchling Beacon is the highest point in the county of East Sussex. Standing at 814 ft (248 m), it is the third largest peak on the South Downs, a range of chalk hills extending 260 square miles.

The summit is accessible using a road that runs from the centre of the village of Ditchling. A large car park can be found at the summit and is owned and operated by the National Trust. The long-distance footpath, the South Downs Way, also passes by the summit. The hill is often used in various charity sporting events which are run between London and Brighton.

LOG

Date:	**Week No:**
Start Point:	**Day:**
Start Time:	**Pace:**
Finish Time:	**Total Ascent:**
Elapsed Time:	**Total Distance:**

⬠ **Height:** 807 ft (246 m) 🌐 **County:** East Riding of Yorkshire

⦿ **Region:** Yorkshire Wolds ◈ **Lat/Long:** 53.9909,-0.75829857

⦾ **Grid Ref:** SE 821 570 🗺 **OS Map:** OS 294

🖼 **Category:** Historic County Top, Current County Top, Marilyn

Bishop Wilton Wold sits at 807 ft (246 m) and is the highest point in the county of East Riding of Yorkshire. It is also the highest point of the Yorkshire Wolds, a set of low-lying chalk hills that span across into North Yorkshire.

Known as Garrowby Hill, the summit sits just north of Bishop Wilton. The A166 passes over the top. A trig point can be found marking the summit. The site was also the scene of a plane crash. On 7 February 1944, an RAF Halifax MkV crashed on the hill during a training flight. The hill has also been made famous by the British artist David Hockney - he painted a view of the summit in 1998.

LOG

Date:	Week No:
Start Point:	Day:
Start Time:	Pace:
Finish Time:	Total Ascent:
Elapsed Time:	Total Distance:

⌂ **Height:** 804 ft (245 m)

○ **Region:** Kent Downs

◎ **Grid Ref:** TQ 436 564

🖼 **Category:** Current County Top, Marilyn

⊕ **County:** Greater London

◈ **Lat/Long:** 51.2894, 0.05835951

🕮 **OS Map:** OS 147

Standing 804 ft (245 m) above sea level, Westerham Heights is the highest point of Greater London. It is also part of Betsom's Hill, Kent's highest point. The top is located next to the A233, along where the county boundary intersects. A tripoint, known as Rag Hill, exists on the north-west side of the hill. This is where the counties of Surrey, Kent, and Greater London all combine.

Interestingly, the A233 was the venue of one of the earliest bicycle hill climbs. In August 1887, twenty-four competitors took part in the hill climb using a variety of bicycles, including penny-farthings. Only half the competitors completed the race.

LOG

Date:	Week No:
Start Point:	Day:
Start Time:	Pace:
Finish Time:	Total Ascent:
Elapsed Time:	Total Distance:

⌂ **Height:** 800 ft (244 m)

⬤ **County:** Hertfordshire

○ **Region:** Aylesbury Vale

◉ **Lat/Long:** 51.7743, -0.67981537

⌖ **Grid Ref:** SP 914 091

▭ **OS Map:** OS 181

▦ **Category:** Historic County Top, Current County Top

Pavis Wood is an area of woodland found at a maximum height of 800 ft (244 m). It is the highest point in the county of Hertfordshire. The wooded plateau is considered an ancient woodland and it contains a wide variety of plants. The woodland is located near the village of Hastoe that sits below the A41.

LOG

Date:	Week No:
Start Point:	Day:
Start Time:	Pace:
Finish Time:	Total Ascent:
Elapsed Time:	Total Distance:

DUNSTABLE DOWNS

△ **Height:** 797 ft (243 m)

⊕ **County:** Bedfordshire

○ **Region:** Chiltern Hills

◉ **Lat/Long:** 51.8642, -0.53638425

◉ **Grid Ref:** TL 008 194

▥ **OS Map:** OS 182

🖼 **Category:** Historic County Top, Current County Top

At 797 ft (243 m), the Dunstable Downs is the highest point in the county of Bedfordshire. The hills are a chalk escarpment, forming the north-eastern area of the Chilterns. Owing to its height, the area is often used by paragliders, kite fliers, and gliders more generally. The home of the London Gliding club can be found at the foot of the hills.

The summit sits next to the B4541 allowing easy access to reach the top where a trig point can be found. Two long-distance paths also pass through the area - the Icknield Way, a unique path that claims to be 'the oldest road in Britain', and the Chiltern Way.

LOG

Date:	**Week No:**
Start Point:	**Day:**
Start Time:	**Pace:**
Finish Time:	**Total Ascent:**
Elapsed Time:	**Total Distance:**

ST BONIFACE DOWN

⌂	**Height:** 790 ft (241 m)	⊕	**County:** Isle of Wight
O	**Region:** Ventnor Downs	◉	**Lat/Long:** 50.6044, -1.19632686
⊙	**Grid Ref:** SZ 569 785	▥	**OS Map:** OL 29
▨	**Category:** Historic County Top, Current County Top, Marilyn, Hardy		

At 790 ft (241 m), St Boniface Down, a chalk down, is the highest point on the Isle of Wight. It is located 1 km from the town of Ventnor and forms part of the significant Ventnor Downs estate. The name 'St Boniface Down' derives from a belief that St Boniface himself (a key player in the Anglo-Saxon mission to the Frankish Empire) preached in Bonchurch at Pulpit Rock in the eighth century.

The top can be reached by walking a short distance from Down Lane, the road running across the Ventnor Downs. A round barrow is positioned at the top. You can also find a radar station depicted in the film 'The Battle of Britain' because the Stuka Bombers dropped bombs on it in 1940.

LOG

Date:	**Week No:**
Start Point:	**Day:**
Start Time:	**Pace:**
Finish Time:	**Total Ascent:**
Elapsed Time:	**Total Distance:**

ARBURY HILL, BIG HILL

⌂ **Height:** 738 ft (225 m)　　⊕ **County:** Northamptonshire

○ **Region:** Daventry　　◉ **Lat/Long:** 52.2244, -1.21061803

⊙ **Grid Ref:** SP 540 587　　▥ **OS Map:** OS 206

🖼 **Category:** Historic County Top, Current County Top

Arbury Hill is 738 ft (225 m) tall and is the highest point in the county of Northamptonshire. Located 5.5 m southwest of the town of Daventry, the slopes sit on a drainage divide between three of the major catchment areas: the River Nene (to the north, south, and east), the river Cherwell (as it feeds into the Thames to the south-west), and to the River Leam (which feeds the River Severn, to the west and north-west).

On the summit of the hill are the remnants of an Iron Age hillfort. It is only visible in the form of a square ditch and embankment stretching 656 ft (200 m) across.

LOG

Date:	Week No:
Start Point:	Day:
Start Time:	Pace:
Finish Time:	Total Ascent:
Elapsed Time:	Total Distance:

SILVERHILL

⛰ **Height:** 670 ft (204 m)   ⊕ **County:** Nottinghamshire

○ **Region:** Ashfield   ◉ **Lat/Long:** 53.1543, -1.2991857

◉ **Grid Ref:** SK 470 621   ▥ **OS Map:** OS 269

🖼 **Category:** Current County Top

At 673 ft (205 m), Silverhill is the tallest, artificial hill in the county of Nottinghamshire. It was originally a mine spoil heap of the former Silverhill Colliery, however, it closed in 1990. In 2005, landscapers added an extra five metres of height to the hilltop.

The flat area of the summit provides panoramic views stretching over five counties. Lincoln Cathedral and Bolsover Castle can be seen from the summit. A bronze statue of a coal miner holding a Davy lamp is located on a rock plinth at a viewpoint on the summit. It is a tribute to all the miners of the Nottinghamshire coalfields.

LOG

Date:	Week No:
Start Point:	Day:
Start Time:	Pace:
Finish Time:	Total Ascent:
Elapsed Time:	Total Distance:

COLD OVERTON PARK

⛰ **Height:** 646 ft (197 m) ⊕ **County:** Rutland

○ **Region:** Cold Overton Park Wood ◈ **Lat/Long:** 52.6695, -0.78390302

⊙ **Grid Ref:** SK 827 085 ▥ **OS Map:** OS 234

🖼 **Category:** Historic County Top, Current County Top

At 646 ft (197 m) high, Cold Overton Park is the highest point in Rutland, the smallest county in the UK. Located near the county town of Oakham, the summit can be reached just off Cold Overton Road – a road that runs between nearby Knossington and Oakham. The hilltop is marked with a trig point pillar, located just to the east of Cold Overton Park Wood.

LOG

Date:		**Week No:**
Start Point:		**Day:**
Start Time:		**Pace:**
Finish Time:		**Total Ascent:**
Elapsed Time:		**Total Distance:**

⌂	**Height:**	587 ft (179 m)	⊕ **County:**	Merseyside
○	**Region:**	St. Helens	◉ **Lat/Long:**	53.5075, -2.71681723
◉	**Grid Ref:**	SD 525 014	▥ **OS Map:**	OS 285
▱	**Category:**	Historic County Top, Current County Top, Marilyn		

Billinge Hill is the highest point in the county of Merseyside. At 587 ft (179 m) it lies in Billinge, a village within the Metropolitan Borough of St Helens. A beacon tower sits at the summit.

A number of footpaths lead to the summit where you can find several large transmitter masts. Views are far-reaching and extend over to Manchester, the Derbyshire Peak District, and to the Blackpool Tower. On a good day, the mountains of Snowdonia can even be seen.

The Royal Observer Corps, a civil defence group, also used the hilltop to aid in the visual detection, identification tracking, and reporting of aircraft over the UK during its years of operation between 1925 and 1995.

LOG

Date:	**Week No:**
Start Point:	**Day:**
Start Time:	**Pace:**
Finish Time:	**Total Ascent:**
Elapsed Time:	**Total Distance:**

NORMANBY HILL (WOLDS TOP)

⌂ **Height:** 551 ft (168 m) ⊕ **County:** Lincolnshire

○ **Region:** Lincolnshire Wolds ◉ **Lat/Long:** 53.453, -0.31317732

◉ **Grid Ref:** TF 121 964 ▥ **OS Map:** OS 284

▥ **Category:** Historic County Top, Current County Top, Marilyn

Normanby Hill, also referred to as Wolds Top, is the highest point in the county of Lincolnshire. It is 551 ft (168 m) high and is situated in the Lincolnshire Wolds, a range of hills running roughly parallel with the North Sea coast.

Normanby le Wold village, home to a delightful small church, is close to the summit. The Viking Way, a 147-mile walking trail between the Humber bridge and Oakham, passes close to the hilltop. The summit is marked with a trig point, erected in 1936.

LOG

Date:	Week No:
Start Point:	Day:
Start Time:	Pace:
Finish Time:	Total Ascent:
Elapsed Time:	Total Distance:

DUNDRY HILL

⌂ **Height:** 525 ft (160 m) ⊕ **County:** Bristol

○ **Region:** North Somerset ◉ **Lat/Long:** 51.4008, -2.61481107

⊙ **Grid Ref:** ST 593 668 ▭ **OS Map:** OS 155

▱ **Category:** Current County Top, Marilyn

Dundry Hill stands at 525 ft (160 m). It is the highest point in Bristol. Located directly south of the city, the summit can be found close to the village of Dundry along with its iconic church. The hill stretches for two miles and is made up of farmland and a small number of buildings.

The eastern side of the hill is located by Maes Knoll, an Iron Age hillfort. It is also near to Wansdyke, a series of medieval earthworks that provide a defensive barrier. On the western side, you can find a spring that forms the Land Yeo, a small river that flows through North Somerset and still powers a functional watermill.

LOG

Date:	**Week No:**
Start Point:	**Day:**
Start Time:	**Pace:**
Finish Time:	**Total Ascent:**
Elapsed Time:	**Total Distance:**

CHRISHALL COMMON

⟁ **Height:**	482 ft (147 m)	⊕ **County:**	Essex
○ **Region:**	Chrishall	◉ **Lat/Long:**	52.0055, 0.10079814
◎ **Grid Ref:**	TL 443 362	▥ **OS Map:**	OS 194
▣ **Category:**	Historic County Top, Current County Top		

Chrishall is a small village that sits at the highest point in the county of Essex. At 482 ft (147 m) above sea level, locals have avoided all road construction around the hill, allowing the village to retain its character. The village, therefore, is off the beaten track but is still fortunate enough to have many facilities.

The village is also presumed to be the place where M.R. James set the short ghost story 'The Story of a Disappearance and an Appearance' (1919).

LOG

Date:		**Week No:**
Start Point:		**Day:**
Start Time:		**Pace:**
Finish Time:		**Total Ascent:**
Elapsed Time:		**Total Distance:**

△ **Height:** 479 ft (146 m)

⊕ **County:** Cambridgeshire

○ **Region:** Great and Little Chishill Parish

◉ **Lat/Long:** 52.027, 0.07908411

◎ **Grid Ref:** TL427386

🗺 **OS Map:** OS 194

🖼 **Category:** Historic County Top, Current County Top

The pleasant village of Great Chishill is part of the civil parish of Great and Little Chisll. It is the highest point of the county of Cambridgeshire and sits 479 ft (146 m) above sea level. The village is roughly one mile east of the Hertfordshire boundary.

The highest point can be found by venturing approximately 800 m east along Hall Lane from St Swithun's parish church. The village is also the place where the famous singer-songwriter Sam Smith grew up, he worked in the local shop in Barley.

LOG

Date:	Week No:
Start Point:	Day:
Start Time:	Pace:
Finish Time:	Total Ascent:
Elapsed Time:	Total Distance:

GREAT WOOD HILL

△ **Height:** 420 ft (128 m)   ⊕ **County:** Suffolk

○ **Region:** Newmarket Ridge   ◉ **Lat/Long:** 52.1162, 1.08672641

⊙ **Grid Ref:** TL 786 558   📖 **OS Map:** OS 210

🖼 **Category:** Historic County Top, Current County Top

Great Wood Hill is the highest point in the county of Suffolk. At 420 ft (128 m), it is also the highest point of the Newmarket Ridge, a ridge approximately 40 miles long that starts in Hertfordshire and ends near Sudbury in Suffolk, passing through Essex and south-east Cambridgeshire along the way.

The top of the hill is situated just south of the village of Chedburgh, off from the A143. It is within a small patch of woodland, reached by a nearby road that runs alongside the wood. A communications mast is located nearby.

LOG

Date:	Week No:
Start Point:	Day:
Start Time:	Pace:
Finish Time:	Total Ascent:
Elapsed Time:	Total Distance:

BEACON HILL

△ **Height:** 338 ft (103 m)

⊕ **County:** Norfolk

○ **Region:** Cromer Ridge

◉ **Lat/Long:** 52.9258, 1.24684322

◉ **Grid Ref:** TG 183 414

▥ **OS Map:** OS 252

🖼 **Category:** Historic County Top, Current County Top

With a height of 344 ft (105 m), Beacon Hill is the highest point in the county of Norfolk. The hill is part of Cromer Ridge, a ridge of old glacial moraines, thought to have been the frontline of the ice sheet during the last ice age.

The area is sometimes known as the Roman Camp, although no evidence of Roman occupation has been found on the site. The name is believed to have been concocted by cab drivers during the nineteenth-century to make it more alluring to tourists.

The hill is located approximately 0.7 miles from the village of West Runton. You can make the ascent to the summit from here.

LOG

Date:	Week No:
Start Point:	Day:
Start Time:	Pace:
Finish Time:	Total Ascent:
Elapsed Time:	Total Distance:

HIGH HOLBORN

△ **Height:** 72 ft (22 m)

○ **Region:** The City

⊙ **Grid Ref:** TQ 309 816

▣ **Category:** Current County Top

⊕ **County:** City of London

⊙ **Lat/Long:** 51.518435 -0.113896

▢ **OS Map:** OS 173

At a mere 72 ft (22 m) above sea level, High Holborn is the highest point in the City of London and the lowest county top in England. The street runs through the Farringdon Without Ward in the western sector of the City.

The nearest underground stations are Holborn and Chancery Lane, both on the central line. Walking between these stations takes you over the flat peak. Landmarks include the Embassy of Cuba and the historic grade II listed Cittie of Yorke public house, near to the city boundary. It should be noted, the current building is actually a rebuild from the 1920s but there has been a pub on this site since 1430.

LOG

Date:		**Week No:**	
Start Point:		**Day:**	
Start Time:		**Pace:**	
Finish Time:		**Total Ascent:**	
Elapsed Time:		**Total Distance:**	

SCOTLAND COUNTY TOPS

Prior to 1996 Scotland had thirty-four designated counties. For purposes of local government, areas were subsequently divided, it now has thirty-two designated unitary authorities. The table is ranked in order of highest county top to the smallest. ☑

1. Highland	☐	2. Aberdeenshire	☐
3. Moray	☐	4. Perth and Kinross	☐
5. Stirling	☐	6. Argyll and Bute	☐
7. Angus	☐	8. North Ayrshire	☐
9. Dumfries and Galloway	☐	10. Scottish Borders	☐
11. Western Isles	☐	12. South Ayrshire	☐
13. South Lanarkshire	☐	14. Clackmannanshire	☐
15. East Ayrshire	☐	16. Midlothian	☐
17. East Dunbartonshire	☐	18. Edinburgh	☐
19. West Lothian	☐	20. East Lothian	☐
21. North Lanarkshire	☐	22. Fife	☐
23. Renfrewshire	☐	24. Orkney Islands	☐
25. Shetland Islands	☐	26. Inverclyde	☐
27. West Dunbartonshire	☐	28. East Renfrewshire	☐
29. Falkirk	☐	30. Aberdeen	☐
31. Glasgow	☐	32. Dundee	☐

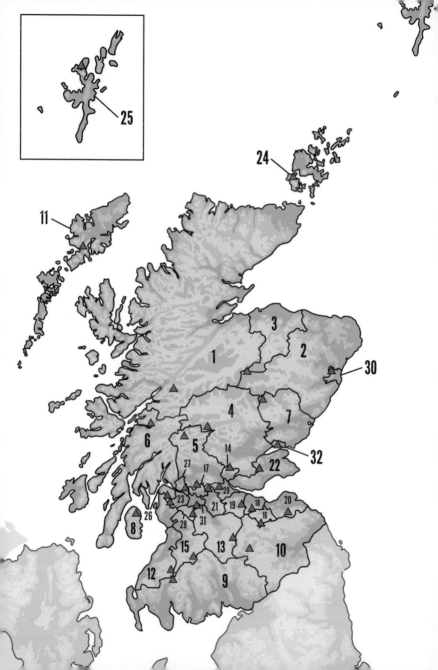

⌂ **Height:**	4,413 ft (1,345 m)	⊕ **County:**	Highland
○ **Region:**	Grampian Mountains	⊕ **Lat/Long:**	56.7968, -5.00328149
⊙ **Grid Ref:**	NN 166 712	▥ **OS Map:**	OS 392
▣ **Category:**	Country High Point, Historic County Top, Current County Top, Munro, Marilyn		

Standing at a height of 4,413 ft (1,345 m), Ben Nevis is famously known for being the highest point in the United Kingdom. Ben Nevis falls within the Grampian Mountains in the county, Highland. It is a popular destination – approximately 100,000 people ascend the summit each year.

The simplest and easiest route to the summit is the Pony Track or Tourist Route. It begins in Achintee, located to the east of Glen Nevis. The top is a collapsed dome of a former volcano and features the ruins of an observatory, formerly staffed between 1883 and 1904.

LOG

Date:	**Week No:**
Start Point:	**Day:**
Start Time:	**Pace:**
Finish Time:	**Total Ascent:**
Elapsed Time:	**Total Distance:**

BEN MACDUI

⌂ **Height:** 4,295 ft (1,309 m)
⊕ **County:** Aberdeenshire / Moray
○ **Region:** Cairngorms
◉ **Lat/Long:** 57.0704, -3.6691058
◉ **Grid Ref:** NN 988 989
▥ **OS Map:** OL 57
🖼 **Category:** Historic County Top, Current County Top, Munro, Marilyn

With an elevation of 4,295 ft (1,309 m), Ben Macdui is the second highest mountain in the United Kingdom and sits within the Cairngorms National Park. The mountain sits on the southern edge of the Cairngorm Plateau which lies on the boundary of Aberdeenshire and Moray. As a result, both counties share the mountain as their highest point.

The easiest ascent to the summit can be made from the Coire Cas car park, located at the base of Cairngorm Ski Centre. The route is approximately 4 miles (7 km) long. Queen Victoria even climbed the summit on the 7th October 1859. A direction indicator sits at the top and highlights the most important hills viewable on a clear day.

LOG

Date:	Week No:
Start Point:	Day:
Start Time:	Pace:
Finish Time:	Total Ascent:
Elapsed Time:	Total Distance:

△	**Height:**	3,983 ft (1,214 m)	**County:**	Perth and Kinross
O	**Region:**	Scottish Highlands	**Lat/Long:**	56.5449, -4.22091595
◎	**Grid Ref:**	NN 636 414	**OS Map:**	OL 48
▨	**Category:**	Historic County Top, Current County Top, Munro, Marilyn

With an elevation of 3,983 ft (1,214 m), Ben Lawers is the highest mountain in the southern area of the Scottish Highlands and the county of Perth and Kinross. It lies to the north of Loch Tay and is the highest of a long ridge that includes seven other Munros.

An ascent to the summit can be made from Ben Lawers car park, located south-east of the mountain. From here, a footpath leads to the summit by way of the peak Beinn Ghlas.

The area is regarded by botanists to be one of the richest areas for alpine flora in the UK. There is an abundance of rare alpine plants, as a result, it is a Special Area of Conservation.

LOG

Date:	**Week No:**
Start Point:	**Day:**
Start Time:	**Pace:**
Finish Time:	**Total Ascent:**
Elapsed Time:	**Total Distance:**

BEN MORE

⛰ **Height:** 3,852 ft (1,174 m) 🌐 **County:** Stirling

◯ **Region:** Crianlarich Hills ◉ **Lat/Long:** 56.386, -4.54012788

◎ **Grid Ref:** NN 432 244 📖 **OS Map:** OL 46

🖼 **Category:** Current County Top, Munro, Marilyn

Ben More has an elevation of 3,852 ft (1,174 m) and is the highest point in the county of Stirling. There is nowhere further south of the UK that is higher. It is also the highest mountain in the Crianlarich Hills, a large group of hills running east of Loch Lomond.

The easiest ascent to the summit starts from Benmore Farm on the A85. From here, a trail leads off at the end of the path and the route continues up the relentlessly steep north-west ridge.

Tragedy stuck on the mountain on 19th January 1973. A Vickers Viscount flew into the side of the mountain, 30 m below the summit. The aircraft had been flying over snow-covered high terrain and had failed to maintain a safe altitude.

LOG

Date:	Week No:
Start Point:	Day:
Start Time:	Pace:
Finish Time:	Total Ascent:
Elapsed Time:	Total Distance:

Height:	3,694 ft (1,126 m)	**County:**	Argyll and Bute
Region:	Cruachan Horseshoe	**Lat/Long:**	56.4268, -5.13195881
Grid Ref:	NN 069 304	**OS Map:**	OS 377
Category:	Current County Top, Munro, Marilyn		

Ben Cruachan, with an elevation of 3,694 ft (1,126 m), is the highest point in the county of Argyll and Bute. The mountain is very popular and forms part of the Cruachan Horseshoe, a ring of mountains that surrounds a nearby dam.

A popular route to the summit is from the car park located next to the visitor's centre, near to the Falls of Cruchan train station. The path leading up is steep and rocky with sections of easy scrambling. Beneath the mountain lies one of the greatest engineering feats in British history: a hydro-electric power station buried 3,280 ft (1 km) underground, generating up to 440MW at peak demand.

LOG

Date:		**Week No:**
Start Point:		**Day:**
Start Time:		**Pace:**
Finish Time:		**Total Ascent:**
Elapsed Time:		**Total Distance:**

GLAS MAOL

⛰ **Height:** 3,504 ft (1,068 m) ⊕ **County:** Angus

○ **Region:** Mounth Hills ⊙ **Lat/Long:** 56.8731, -3.36825949

◎ **Grid Ref:** NO 167 765 🗺 **OS Map:** OL 52

🖼 **Category:** Historic County Top, Current County Top, Munro, Marilyn

Glas Maol stands at 3,504 ft (1,068 m). Although the flat summit is shared between Aberdeenshire, Angus and Perth, and Kinross, the highest point lies in Angus, making it the highest point in this county.

A layby can be found just off the A39, the highest public road in Scotland, located to the west of the mountain. Due to the high level of the road, this route makes for an easier ascent. The western slopes are also home to the Clenshee Ski Centre, the largest ski resort in Scotland.

LOG

Date:	Week No:
Start Point:	Day:
Start Time:	Pace:
Finish Time:	Total Ascent:
Elapsed Time:	Total Distance:

GOAT FELL

⌂ **Height:** 2,867 ft (874 m)   ⊕ **County:** North Ayrshire

○ **Region:** Corbetts   ⊙ **Lat/Long:** 55.6258, -5.19197765

⊚ **Grid Ref:** NR 991 415   ▥ **OS Map:** OS 361

▦ **Category:** Historic County Top, Current County Top, Marilyn, Hardy

Goat Fell (Gaoda Bheinn) stands at 2,867 ft (874 m) and is the highest point on the Isle of Arran, which falls within the county of North Ayrshire. This mountain is part of the four Corbett. Along with nearby Brodick Castle, it is now owned by the National Trust for Scotland.

The island remains very popular with tourists, therefore, Goat Fell is a very popular peak. There are several possible routes you can take to reach the summit. The most commonly used route starts near Brodick Castle in Cladach and follows along a constructed path for 3 miles. A short, steeper route can be made from the village of Corrie.

LOG

Date:	Week No:
Start Point:	Day:
Start Time:	Pace:
Finish Time:	Total Ascent:
Elapsed Time:	Total Distance:

MERRICK

⌂ **Height:** 2,766 ft (843 m)   ⊕ **County:** Dumfries and Galloway

○ **Region:** Southern Uplands   ◉ **Lat/Long:** 55.1393, -4.46842887

⊙ **Grid Ref:** NX 427 855   ▥ **OS Map:** OS 318

▨ **Category:** Historic County Top, Current County Top, Marilyn

Merrick (Mearaig), standing at 2,766 ft (843 m), is the highest mountain in the county of Dumfries and Galloway. It falls within the Range of the Awful Hand, a range of five hills named after their resemblance to the fingers of a hand.

The shortest ascent to the top is from the car park located in Glen Trool, near to Bruce's Stone. Bruce's Stone is a monument that commemorates the victory of Robert the Bruce over the English in 1307. Fortunately, you know when you have reached the summit as you will find a trig point at the top. Views extend from the peak over towards the Lake District fells, the Isle of Man, and the Northern Coast of Ireland.

LOG

Date:	Week No:
Start Point:	Day:
Start Time:	Pace:
Finish Time:	Total Ascent:
Elapsed Time:	Total Distance:

⚇ **Height:** 2,760 ft (840 m) ⊕ **County:** Scottish Borders

⭘ **Region:** Southern Uplands ◉ **Lat/Long:** 55.7722, -3.0462252

⊚ **Grid Ref:** NT 146 235 ▥ **OS Map:** OS 345

🖼 **Category:** Historic County Top, Current County Top, Marilyn

Broad Law stands at 2,760 ft (840 m) and is the highest point in the county of the Scottish Borders located in the Southern Uplands, the least populous area of mainland Scotland.

The broad, rounded summit can be reached from any of the surrounding villages, although Megget Stone, south of the mountain, provides a good starting point. An air traffic beacon and nearby radio tower mark the top of the mountain.

LOG

Date:	Week No:
Start Point:	Day:
Start Time:	Pace:
Finish Time:	Total Ascent:
Elapsed Time:	Total Distance:

AN CLISEAM

⌂ **Height:** 2,621 ft (799 m) ⊕ **County:** Na h-Eileanan Siar

O **Region:** Outer Hebrides ◉ **Lat/Long:** 57.9637, -6.81255564

◉ **Grid Ref:** NB 154 073 ▥ **OS Map:** OS 456

🖼 **Category:** Current County Top, Marilyn, Corbett

Clisham sits at an elevation of 2,621 ft (799 m). It is the highest mountain in the Outer Hebrides and falls within the county of the Western Isles. It is the only mountain in the archipelago that is categorised as a Corbett.

The easiest route to reach to the summit is from the highest point of the A859 road that runs between Tarbet and Ardvourlie.When you reach the top, you are rewarded with fantastic views out to sea and over the surrounding mountains.

LOG

Date:	Week No:
Start Point:	Day:
Start Time:	Pace:
Finish Time:	Total Ascent:
Elapsed Time:	Total Distance:

KIRRIEREOCH HILL

⌂ **Height:** 2,579 ft (786 m)   ⊕ **County:** South Ayrshire

○ **Region:** Southern Uplands ◉ **Lat/Long:** 55.152508, -4.480328

◉ **Grid Ref:** NX 420 870   ▥ **OS Map:** OS 318

▨ **Category:** Historic County Top, Current County Top

Kirriereoch Hill (Coire Riabhach) has an elevation of 2,579 ft (786 m) and sits in the Range of the Awful, Southern Upland Hills. It sits in the same range to that of Merrick, the county top of Dumfries and Galloway.

The shortest ascent to the top is from the car park located in Glentrool, near Bruce's Stone. The latter being a monument to commemorate the victory of Robert the Bruce over the English in 1307.

LOG

Date:	Week No:
Start Point:	Day:
Start Time:	Pace:
Finish Time:	Total Ascent:
Elapsed Time:	Total Distance:

CULTER FELL

⟁ **Height:** 2,454 ft (748 m)　　⊕ **County:** South Lanarkshire

○ **Region:** Culter Hills　　◉ **Lat/Long:** 55.5462, -3.5027225

◎ **Grid Ref:** NT 052 290　　▥ **OS Map:** OS 336

🖼 **Category:** Historic County Top, Current County Top, Marilyn

Culter Fell has an elevation of 2,454 ft (748 m). It is the highest point in the county of South Lanarkshire and is the highest out of the Culter Hills, a culmination of ridges that lie to the south of the village Coulter.

Much of the mountain can be accessed via narrow roads and tracks. The easiest ascent can be made from Culter Allers Farm, located to the north-west of the mountain, where a continuously steep climb leads to the top. On a clear day, with good visibility, views stretch between the Cumbrian Lake District to the Scottish Highlands.

LOG

Date:	**Week No:**
Start Point:	**Day:**
Start Time:	**Pace:**
Finish Time:	**Total Ascent:**
Elapsed Time:	**Total Distance:**

BEN CLEUCH

⌂	**Height:**	2,365 ft (721 m)	⊕ **County:**	Clackmannanshire
○	**Region:**	Ochil Hills	◉ **Lat/Long:**	56.1857, -3.76951179
◎	**Grid Ref:**	NN 902 006	▥ **OS Map:**	OL 46

🖼 **Category:** Historic County Top, Current County Top, Marilyn

Ben Cleuch stands at 2,365 ft (721 m). It is the highest point in the county of Clackmannanshire and sits within the Ochil Hills, a range of hills north of the Forth Valley. It is one of the most popular hill walks in central Scotland.

There are many possible routes to the summit. The easiest route starts at Mill St, Tillicoultry, just south of the summit along the A91. A trig point set within a stone shelter marks the peak. With good visibility, views stretch far to the north and south, with the Forth bridges and Edinburgh visible on a good day.

LOG

Date:	**Week No:**
Start Point:	**Day:**
Start Time:	**Pace:**
Finish Time:	**Total Ascent:**
Elapsed Time:	**Total Distance:**

BLACKCRAIG HILL

⛰ **Height:** 2,296 ft (700 m)

🌐 **County:** East Ayrshire

⭕ **Region:** Carsphairn Hills

◈ **Lat/Long:** 55.3335, -4.13403024

📍 **Grid Ref:** NS 647 064

📖 **OS Map:** OS 328

🖼 **Category:** Current County Top, Marilyn

Blackcraig Hill stands at 2,296 ft (700 m). It is the highest point in the county of East Ayrshire. A number of other hills can be found in the area.

You can reach the summit from a small parking area at Blackcraig Farm, north from Afton Reservoir. This route leads from the farm directly up the north face of the hill. A trig point and a number of cairns mark the summit.

LOG

Date:	Week No:
Start Point:	Day:
Start Time:	Pace:
Finish Time:	Total Ascent:
Elapsed Time:	Total Distance:

BLACKHOPE SCAR

⏒ **Height:**	2,135 ft (651 m)	⊕ **County:**	Midlothian
⭘ **Region:**	Moorfoot Hills	◎ **Lat/Long:**	55.7236, -3.09169754
⦿ **Grid Ref:**	NT 315 483	▥ **OS Map:**	OS 337
▤ **Category:**	Historic County Top, Current County Top, Marilyn

Blackhope Scar has an elevation of 2,135 ft (651 m). It is the highest point in the county of Midlothian. The hill is situated in the Moorfoot Hills, a range of hills located to the south of Edinburgh. The government has designated this section as a Special Area of Conservation.

A popular route to the summit can be found from the nearby Gladhouse Reservoir. A trig point is situated at the top of the hill next to a fence.

LOG

Date:	**Week No:**
Start Point:	**Day:**
Start Time:	**Pace:**
Finish Time:	**Total Ascent:**
Elapsed Time:	**Total Distance:**

EARL'S SEAT

⏚ **Height:** 1,896 ft (578 m)   ⊕ **County:** East Dunbartonshire

○ **Region:** Campsie Fells   ◎ **Lat/Long:** 56.0257, -4.29637856

◎ **Grid Ref:** NS 569 838   ▥ **OS Map:** OS 348

🖼 **Category:** Current County Top, Marilyn

Standing at 1,896 ft (578m), Earl's seat is the highest point in the county of East Dunbartonshire. The hill is situated within Campsie Fells, a range of hills that lie between the river Endrick Water and the valley of Strathblane.

A route to the summit that incorporates nearby hills Holehead, Hart Hill, and Hog Hill, can be made from a parking area north-west of Balgrochan on the B822. It is rumoured that the English scientist Michel Faraday came up with the theory of electromagnetic induction while lost on the Fells. The summit is marked by a trig point.

LOG

Date:	Week No:
Start Point:	Day:
Start Time:	Pace:
Finish Time:	Total Ascent:
Elapsed Time:	Total Distance:

EAST CAIRN HILL

⌂ **Height:** 1,860 ft (567 m)   ⊕ **County:** Edinburgh

○ **Region:** Pentland Hills   ◉ **Lat/Long:** 55.8192, -3.39313126

⊙ **Grid Ref:** NT 128 593   ▥ **OS Map:** OS 344

🖻 **Category:** Current County Top, Marilyn

East Cairn hill sits at an elevation of 1,860 ft (567m). It is the highest point in the council district of Edinburgh and it forms part of the Pentland Hills, a 20-mile range of hills south-west of Edinburgh.

To reach the summit, a road leads off from Baddinsgill Farm, located south and near to Baddinsgill Reservoir. The track leads up to the summit of Little Hill, you can then find East Cairn Hill just further north-east of here. A round cairn sits at the summit measuring 55 ft in diameter and 6 ft high. Views extend over the main Pentland Range.

LOG

Date:	Week No:
Start Point:	Day:
Start Time:	Pace:
Finish Time:	Total Ascent:
Elapsed Time:	Total Distance:

WEST CAIRN HILL

⌂ **Height:** 1,843 ft (562 m)

⊕ **County:** West Lothian

○ **Region:** Pentland Hills

◉ **Lat/Long:** 55.8103, -3.42625077

◉ **Grid Ref:** NT 107 583

▥ **OS Map:** OS 344

🖼 **Category:** Current County Top

With an elevation of 1,843 ft (562 m), West Cairn Hill is the highest point of the county of West Lothian. It forms one of the Pentland Hills, a range of hills that stretch 15 miles from the foothills of Edinburgh to Newbigging and Dunsyre. It is the highest point in the county of West Lothian.

You can ascend to the summit from Harperrig Reservoir. Originally built in 1860, this reservoir sits close to the A70. Here, a number of trails lead up the mountain. A trig point marks the summit along where a border wall runs.

LOG

Date:	Week No:
Start Point:	Day:
Start Time:	Pace:
Finish Time:	Total Ascent:
Elapsed Time:	Total Distance:

MEIKLE SAYS LAW

⌂ **Height:**	1,755 ft (535 m)	⊕ **County:**	East Lothian
○ **Region:**	Lammermuir Hills	◉ **Lat/Long:**	55.847, -2.6704196
⊙ **Grid Ref:**	NT 581 617	▥ **OS Map:**	OS 345
▣ **Category:**	Historic County Top, Current County Top, Marilyn		

Meikle Says Law is the highest point in the county of East Lothian, with an elevation of 1,755 ft (535m). It is situated in the Lammermuir hills, a hill range forming a natural boundary between Lothian and the Borders.

The walk to the flat plateau of the summit starts from the minor road at Redstone Rig, just off the B6355. Here, a track leads to the hilltop, marked by a trig point.

LOG

Date:		**Week No:**
Start Point:		**Day:**
Start Time:		**Pace:**
Finish Time:		**Total Ascent:**
Elapsed Time:		**Total Distance:**

CORT-MA LAW EAST TOP

⌂ **Height:** 1,726 ft (526 m) ⊕ **County:** North Lanarkshire

○ **Region:** Campsie Fells ◉ **Lat/Long:** 55.9935,-4.16360179

◎ **Grid Ref:** NS 660 805 ▥ **OS Map:** OS 348

🖼 **Category:** Current County Top

Cort-ma Law East Top sits just to the north-east of the Cort-Ma Law summit. With an elevation of 1,726 ft (526 m), it is the highest point in the county of North Lanarkshire. It is situated east of Earl's Seat, the highest of the Campsie Fells, a range of gently rolling hills in central Scotland.

A route to the top can be made from the car park located at the bend of Crow Road (B822), west of the summit and north of Lennoxtown.

LOG

Date:	Week No:
Start Point:	Day:
Start Time:	Pace:
Finish Time:	Total Ascent:
Elapsed Time:	Total Distance:

WEST LOMOND

⌂ **Height:** 1,713 ft (522 m)   ⊕ **County:** Fife

○ **Region:** Lomond Hills   ⊙ **Lat/Long:** 56.2455, -3.29686983

⊙ **Grid Ref:** NO 197 066   ▥ **OS Map:** OS 370

▱ **Category:** Historic County Top, Current County Top, Marilyn

West Lomond, with an elevation of 1,713 ft (522 m), is the highest point in the county of Fife. Its ridge is located above an escarpment, this makes the peaks of both West Lomond and its neighbour East Lomond visible for miles around.

The summit can be climbed from the car park located at Craigmead on Falkland-Leslie road. A solid trail leads you just to below the summit. On the summit, you can find the remains of an Iron Age Hillfort.

LOG

Date:	Week No:
Start Point:	Day:
Start Time:	Pace:
Finish Time:	Total Ascent:
Elapsed Time:	Total Distance:

HILL OF STAKE

- ⛰ **Height:** 1,712 ft (522 m)
- 🌐 **County:** Renfrewshire
- ⭕ **Region:** Clyde Muirshiel
- ◉ **Lat/Long:** 55.8293, -4.757963
- 📍 **Grid Ref:** NS 273 630
- 🗺 **OS Map:** OS 341
- 🖼 **Category:** Historic County Top, Current County Top, Marilyn

Hill of Stake has an elevation of 1712 ft (522 m). It is the highest hill in the relatively low-lying county of Renfrewshire. It forms part of the Clyde Muirshiel Regional Park, a 108 square mile area of countryside set aside for conservation and recreation.

You can reach the summit from the Murishiel Visitor Centre. You will proceed to trek across wild open moorland, once frequented by former Prime Minister, Winston Churchill. The area has also been the scene of numerous air crashes with a Spartan Cruiser, Hurricane, and Seafire crashing into the side of the hill.

LOG

Date:	Week No:
Start Point:	Day:
Start Time:	Pace:
Finish Time:	Total Ascent:
Elapsed Time:	Total Distance:

WARD HILL

⛰ **Height:** 1,578 ft (481 m)   🌐 **County:** Orkney Islands

⭘ **Region:** Hoy   ◉ **Lat/Long:** 58.9006, -3.34050069

📍 **Grid Ref:** HY 228 022   📖 **OS Map:** OS 462

🖼 **Category:** Historic County Top, Current County Top, Marilyn

---

With an elevation of 1,578 ft (481 m), Ward Hill is the highest point in Hoy, an island located in Orkney. Lying on the north of Hoy island, the hill forms a curved ridge. The lower slopes are covered in sandy soil and littered with small stones.

You can reach the summit from Moaness Pier, the location from which the ferry crossing arrives from Stromness. A trig point crowns the top and offers great views over the Orkney's.

LOG

Date:	**Week No:**
Start Point:	**Day:**
Start Time:	**Pace:**
Finish Time:	**Total Ascent:**
Elapsed Time:	**Total Distance:**

RONAS HILL

⛰ **Height:** 1,480 ft (450 m) ⊕ **County:** Shetland Islands

○ **Region:** Shetland Mainland ⊙ **Lat/Long:** 60.5339, -1.44552636

◉ **Grid Ref:** HU 305 834 ▥ **OS Map:** OS 469

🖾 **Category:** Historic County Top, Current County Top, Marilyn

---

Rising as a stony dome of granite tundra, Ronas Hill stands 1,480 ft (450 m) above sea level and is the highest point of the Shetland Islands. The surrounding landscape provides a wild and windswept existence, with a sub-arctic climate. It is also a Ramsar site and contains many rare Arctic plants.

A parking area can be found atop Collafirth Hill, making for a high-altitude starting point. At the top of Ronas hill, there is a Neolithic Chambered Cairn, unusual in its position owing to its height.

In exceptionally good weather, most of the island can be seen. Views extend as far as the Fair Isle, an island famous for both its bird wildlife and knitwear.

LOG

Date:	Week No:
Start Point:	Day:
Start Time:	Pace:
Finish Time:	Total Ascent:
Elapsed Time:	Total Distance:

CREUCH HILL

△ **Height:** 1,440 ft (439 m) ⊕ **County:** Inverclyde

○ **Region:** Central Lowlands ◉ **Lat/Long:** 55.8831, -4.76730998

◉ **Grid Ref:** NS 265 685 ▥ **OS Map:** OS 341

▣ **Category:** Current County Top

With an elevation of 1,440 ft (439 m), Creuch Hill is the highest hill in the county of Inverclyde. The hill is located in Clyde Muirshiel Regional Park, a collective area set aside for recreation and conservation. The park is also home to the Hill of Stake, the county top of Renfrewshire.

A route to the summit can be made up the western side of the hill by following the road that runs south from Loch Thom.

LOG

Date:	Week No:
Start Point:	Day:
Start Time:	Pace:
Finish Time:	Total Ascent:
Elapsed Time:	Total Distance:

DUNCOLM

⛰ **Height:** 1,315 ft (401 m)　　🌐 **County:** West Dunbartonshire

⭕ **Region:** Kilpatrick Hills　　◉ **Lat/Long:** 55.966, -4.45151254

📍 **Grid Ref:** NS 470 774　　📖 **OS Map:** OL 38

🖼 **Category:** Current County Top, Marilyn

Duncolm, whose name means the Fort of Columba, has an elevation of 1,315 ft (401 m). It is the highest point in the county of West Dunbartonshire. It is located near Loch Humphrey and lies in the Kilpatrick Hills, a range of hills stretching from Dumbarton to Strathblane.

A route to the summit can be made from Kilpatrick Braes car park, located at the south of the mountain. This route passes over two other peaks: Little Duncolm and Middle Duncolm.

LOG

Date:	**Week No:**
Start Point:	**Day:**
Start Time:	**Pace:**
Finish Time:	**Total Ascent:**
Elapsed Time:	**Total Distance:**

CORSE HILL

⌂ **Height:**	1,234 ft (376 m)	⊕ **County:**	East Renfrewshire
◯ **Region:**	Whitelee Forest	◉ **Lat/Long:**	55.6914, -4.23134796
⊙ **Grid Ref:**	NS 598 464	▥ **OS Map:**	OS 334
▨ **Category:**	Current County Top, Marilyn		

Corse Hill stands at 1,234 ft (376 m) and is that highest point in the county of East Renfrewshire. The hilltop sits in the heart of Whitelee Wind Farm.

You can reach the summit from Whitelee Windfarm Visitors Centre, located directly south of Glasgow. There are many, well-maintained tracks that lead all around the area and to its summit. A trig point can be found at the summit, a mere 20 m from wind turbine number 104.

LOG

Date:	**Week No:**
Start Point:	**Day:**
Start Time:	**Pace:**
Finish Time:	**Total Ascent:**
Elapsed Time:	**Total Distance:**

DARRACH HILL

⛰ **Height:** 1171 ft (357 m)   ⊕ **County:** Falkirk

○ **Region:** Kilsyth Hills   ◉ **Lat/Long:** 56.0213, -4.00092137

◎ **Grid Ref:** NS 753 827   ▥ **OS Map:** OS 349

🖼 **Category:** Current County Top

Darrach Hill has an elevation of 1,171 ft (357 m) and is located in the county of Falkirk. Despite its small size, it remains prominent to the local area. It also lies very close to the county borders of North Lanarkshire (to the east) and Stirling (to the north).

A suitable starting point to reach the summit can be found at the car park along Tak-Ma-Doon Road as it runs to the west of the hill between the B818 and the A803.

LOG

Date:	Week No:
Start Point:	Day:
Start Time:	Pace:
Finish Time:	Total Ascent:
Elapsed Time:	Total Distance:

⌂	**Height:**	873 ft (266 m)	⊕ **County:**	Aberdeen
○	**Region:**	Aberdeen City	◉ **Lat/Long:**	57.173, -2.23995107
⊙	**Grid Ref:**	NJ 855 091	▥ **OS Map:**	OS 406
▨	**Category:**	Current County Top, Marilyn		

Brimmond Hill has an elevation of 873 ft (266 m). It is the highest point in the council area of Aberdeen. The hill sits in Brimmond Country Park, west of the city of Aberdeen.

A car park can be found north of the hilltop. A fenced-off road leads up to the summit. The top is home to several transmitter sites and the communication masts present provide direct links between North Sea Oil platforms and their Aberdeen headquarters. Views from the top stretch over the city of Aberdeen.

LOG

Date:	**Week No:**
Start Point:	**Day:**
Start Time:	**Pace:**
Finish Time:	**Total Ascent:**
Elapsed Time:	**Total Distance:**

CATHKIN BRAES

⛰ **Height:** 656 ft (200 m)

🌐 **County:** Glasgow

⭕ **Region:** Cathkin Braes

◎ **Lat/Long:** 55.7976, -4.21164624

📍 **Grid Ref:** NS 614 582

📖 **OS Map:** OS 342

🖼 **Category:** Current County Top

At its highest point, Cathkin Braes stands at 656 ft (200m). It lies to the south-east of Glasgow near the districts of Castlemilk, Fernhill, and Burnside with Carmunnock to the east.

The area is a wooded country park and attracts a lot of mountain bikers. There are a number of mountain bike trails that weave through the area. In 2014, the trails were used as the mountain bike venue for the Commonwealth Games. A car park can be found near the hilltop just off the B759.

LOG

Date:	Week No:
Start Point:	Day:
Start Time:	Pace:
Finish Time:	Total Ascent:
Elapsed Time:	Total Distance:

GALLOW HILL

△ **Height:** 584 ft (178 m)　　⊕ **County:** Dundee

○ **Region:** Templeton Woods◉ **Lat/Long:** 56.4955, -3.03430097

⊚ **Grid Ref:** NO 364 341　　▥ **OS Map:** OS 380

▣ **Category:** Current County Top

Gallow Hill has an elevation of 1,240 ft (378 m) and sits within the council area of Dundee. It forms part of the Dislaw range, a range of hills that extend 30 miles from Forfar in the northeast to Kinnoull Hill near Perth.

The hilltop sits at the north-west of the city of Dundee, a short distance from Downfield Golf Club. Templeton Woods Car Park is located to the west and offers a short walk to the summit where you can find a water tower sitting among the woodland.

LOG

Date:	Week No:
Start Point:	Day:
Start Time:	Pace:
Finish Time:	Total Ascent:
Elapsed Time:	Total Distance:

WALES COUNTY TOPS

In 1996, the Welsh government divided Wales into twenty-two principle areas. The following table is ranked in order of highest county top to the smallest.

☑

1.	Gwynedd	☐	2.	Conwy	☐
3.	Powys	☐	4.	Denbighshire	☐
5.	Wrexham	☐	6.	Carmarthenshire	☐
7.	Ceredigion	☐	8.	Monmouthshire	☐
9.	Neath Port Talbot	☐	10.	Rhondda Cynon Taff	☐
11.	Blaenau Gwent	☐	12.	Torfaen	☐
13.	Bridgend	☐	14.	Flintshire	☐
15.	Pembrokeshire	☐	16.	Caerphilly	☐
17.	Merthyr Tydfil	☐	18.	Swansea	☐
19.	Newport	☐	20.	Cardiff	☐
21.	Isle of Anglesey	☐	22.	Vale of Glamorgan	☐

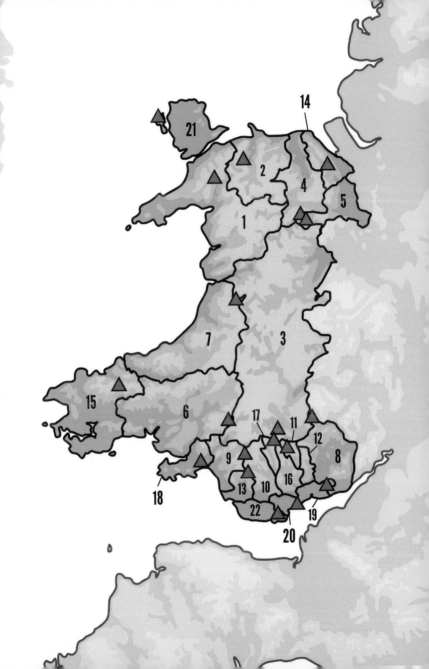

SNOWDON

⌂ **Height:**	3,560 ft (1,085 m)	⊕ **County:**	Gwynedd
○ **Region:**	Snowdonia	◉ **Lat/Long:**	53.0685, -4.07623927
⊙ **Grid Ref:**	SH 609 543	▥ **OS Map:**	OL 17
▣ **Category:**	Country High Point, Current County Top, Marilyn, Hewitt, Nuttall		

Snowdon (Yr Wyddfa), which in old English means "Snow Hill", stands at 3,560 ft (1,085 m) and is the highest mountain in Wales and the highest mountain in the UK outside of Scotland. It remains the busiest peak in the whole of the UK with half a million visitors annually.

There are a number of paths that can be used to reach the summit. At the summit, a café and mountain railway station can be found. Be mindful as the railway operates on a seasonal timetable. More information on the mountain railway can be found by visiting the link below:

(**www.snowdonrailway.co.uk**)

LOG

Date:	Week No:
Start Point:	Day:
Start Time:	Pace:
Finish Time:	Total Ascent:
Elapsed Time:	Total Distance:

CARNEDD LLEWELYN

⛰ **Height:** 3,491 ft (1,064 m)   ⊕ **County:** Conwy

○ **Region:** Snowdonia   ◉ **Lat/Long:** 53.1602, -3.97035151

◉ **Grid Ref:** SH 683 643   🗺 **OS Map:** OL 17

🖼 **Category:** Current County Top, Marilyn, Hewitt, Nuttall

Carnedd Llewelyn, at 3,491 ft (1,064 m), is the highest point in the Carenddau mountain range located in Snowdonia. It sits on the border between Conwy and Gwynedd and is the second highest mountain in Wales by relative height, and the 49th highest in the United Kingdom.

Regardless of your chosen route, every possible trail the summit requires a long walk - it is regarded as one of the most difficult ascents in the country. The summit's boulder-strewn plateau accumulates significant amounts of snow too. Long-lying snow patches have been known to survive through until July.

LOG

Date:	Week No:
Start Point:	Day:
Start Time:	Pace:
Finish Time:	Total Ascent:
Elapsed Time:	Total Distance:

PEN Y FAN

Height: 2,907 ft (886 m) **County:** Powys

Region: Brecon Beacons **Lat/Long:** 51.8839, -3.43709184

Grid Ref: SO 011 215 **OS Map:** OL 12

Category: Historic County Top, Current County Top, Marilyn, Hewitt, Nuttall

At 2,907 ft (886 m) in height, Pen y Fan, located in the Brecon Beacons is the highest point in South Wales. The surrounding area is owned by the National Trust; they manage and repair the area to help combat erosion.

The summit can be reached by heading along the evenly graded footpath that leads from the Storey Arms on the A470. As a result, it is a good mountain to climb during adverse weather conditions.

The mountain is famously used during the selection process for the UK's Special Forces. Named the Fan Dance, recruits are set out on a 15-mile load-bearing march over the peak.

LOG

Date:	Week No:
Start Point:	Day:
Start Time:	Pace:
Finish Time:	Total Ascent:
Elapsed Time:	Total Distance:

CADAIR BERWYN

⛰ **Height:** 2,723 ft (832 m)　🌐 **County:** Denbighshire

⭕ **Region:** Berwyn range　◎ **Lat/Long:** 52.8806, -3.38099016

◉ **Grid Ref:** SJ 071 323　🗺 **OS Map:** OS 255

🖼 **Category:** Historic County Top, Current County Top, Marilyn, Hewitt, Nuttall

Cadair Berwyn stands at 2,723 ft (832 m). It is situated in the north-east of Wales and is the highest point of the Berwyn Range, a sparsely populated area of moorland in Denbighshire. The mountain holds the title of the highest peak outside of Britain's National Parks.

You can reach the summit from the parking lot located at Tan-y-pistyll café. Tan-y-pistyll is also home to the spectacular Pistyll Rhaeadr waterfall, the tallest waterfall in the UK outside of Scotland. A standing stone can be found near to the summit that was re-erected in 2008.

The location was made famous thanks to an apparent UFO-landing that happened in the area on 23 January 1974. It has subsequently come to be known as the 'Berwyn Mountain UFO Incident' and is believed to have been a bright meteor that was widely observed over Wales and northern England at the time.

LOG

Date:	Week No:
Start Point:	Day:
Start Time:	Pace:
Finish Time:	Total Ascent:
Elapsed Time:	Total Distance:

⌂ **Height:** 2,591 ft (790 m)　　⊕ **County:** Wrexham

○ **Region:** Berwyn range　　◎ **Lat/Long:** 52.891836, -3.3733599

◉ **Grid Ref:** SJ 077 335　　▥ **OS Map:** OS 255

🖼 **Category:** Current County Top

Craig Berwyn, with a height of 2,591 ft (790 m), is situated in north-east Wales, alongside its neighbour Cadair Berwyn. The mountain lies on the main ridge that runs north to south in the Berwyn region. Despite Craig Berwyn's proximity to Cadair Berwyn, the mountain falls in the county of Wrexham.

Although there are no obvious features on the summit, you can reach it by heading up to Cadair Berwyn from the car parking area located at Tan-y-pistyll café. Tan-y-pistyl is also home to the spectacular Pistyll Rhaeadr waterfall, the tallest waterfall in the UK outside Scotland. You will find Craig Berwyn's summit approximately 0.4 miles along the ridge line north of Cadair Berwyn.

LOG

Date:	Week No:
Start Point:	Day:
Start Time:	Pace:
Finish Time:	Total Ascent:
Elapsed Time:	Total Distance:

FAN FOEL

⛰ **Height:** 2,562 ft (781 m) ⊕ **County:** Carmarthenshire

○ **Region:** Brecon Beacons ◉ **Lat/Long:** 51.8872, -3.71383007

◉ **Grid Ref:** SN 821 223 ▥ **OS Map:** OL 12

🖾 **Category:** Historic County Top, Current County Top

Fan Foal, coming in at 2,562 ft (781 m), sits north-west of the main summit Fan Brycheiniog within the Brecon Beacons. It is the highest point in the county of Carmarthenshire. Fan Foal, along with two other peaks, form the Carmarthen Fan. The Beacons Way, a 95-mile-long distance footpath, cuts across its summit. The peak is a prominent landmark as it offers panoramic views stretching over the moorland below.

A burial cairn, dating back to the Bronze Age, can be found at the summit. Archaeologists excavated the area between 2002 and 2004 and found that the round barrow contained two separate burials, one with the burnt bones of a woman and two children, and the other with a collared urn and a rare artefact, indicating the possibility of a wealthy person.

LOG

Date:	Week No:
Start Point:	Day:
Start Time:	Pace:
Finish Time:	Total Ascent:
Elapsed Time:	Total Distance:

⚐ **Height:** 2,467 ft (752 m) ⊕ **County:** Ceredigion

○ **Region:** Cambrian Mountains ⊕ **Lat/Long:** 52.467, -3.78308001

⊙ **Grid Ref:** SN 789 869 ▥ **OS Map:** OS 213

▣ **Category:** Historic County Top, Current County Top, Marilyn, Hewitt, Nuttall

Plynlimon (Pumlumon), meaning Five Peaks, stands at a height of 2,467 ft (752 m). It is the highest point of the Cambrian Mountains and also the highest point in Mid Wales. The massif dominates the northern area of the county of Ceredigion.

The peaks that make up the mountain are: Pen Pumlumon Arwystli, Y Garn, Pen Pumlumon Llygad-bychan, and Pumlumon Fach. It is also home to the largest watershed in Wales and the source of the longest river in the UK, the 220-mile River Severn, as well as the origin of the Rheidol and Wye. Folklore states that a sleeping giant even lays beneath Plynlimon.

LOG

Date:	Week No:
Start Point:	Day:
Start Time:	Pace:
Finish Time:	Total Ascent:
Elapsed Time:	Total Distance:

CHWAREL Y FAN

⛰ **Height:** 2,228 ft (679 m)   ⊕ **County:** Monmouthshire

◯ **Region:** Black Mountains   ◉ **Lat/Long:** 51.9576, -3.07981335

◉ **Grid Ref:** SO 259 292   🗺 **OS Map:** OL 13

🖼 **Category:** Historic County Top, Current County Top, Hewitt, Nuttall

Chwarel y Fan is located in the Black Mountains to the south-east of Wales. At 2,2287 ft (679 m), it is the highest point in the county of Monmouthshire. The top forms part of a ridgeline that extends south-eastwards from Rhos Dirion to Bâl Mawr.

The summit can be reached from the car park found at Llanthony Priory. Here, the path leads northwards through the Vale of Ewyas to Capel-y-ffin where the trail then rises steadily up to the thin ridged summit where a cairn can be found.

LOG

Date:	Week No:
Start Point:	Day:
Start Time:	Pace:
Finish Time:	Total Ascent:
Elapsed Time:	Total Distance:

CRAIG Y LLYN

⛰ **Height:** 1968 ft (600 m)

🌐 **County:** Neath Port Talbot / Rhondda Cynon Taff

◯ **Region:** Cynon Valley

◎ **Lat/Long:** 51.7164, -3.58376253

📍 **Grid Ref:** SN 906 031

🗺 **OS Map:** OL 23

🖼 **Category:** Historic County Top, Current County Top

Craig y Llyn has an elevation of 2,000 ft (600 m). It is situated in Rhigos in the Cynon Valley and is located on the boundary of Neath Port Talbot county and Rhondda Cynon Taff county. Both counties share the summit as their highest point.

The hill sits amongst a windfarm but numerous parking areas can be found nearby. With the exception of the north and north-east facing sides, the hill is covered in forest. A trig point can be found at the summit.

LOG

Date:	Week No:
Start Point:	Day:
Start Time:	Pace:
Finish Time:	Total Ascent:
Elapsed Time:	Total Distance:

COITY MOUNTAIN

⛰ **Height:**   1,896 ft (578 m)   🌐 **County:**   Torfaen / Blaenau Gwent

⭕ **Region:**   Brecon Beacons   ◉ **Lat/Long:**   51.7653, -3.11474693

📍 **Grid Ref:**   SO 231 079   📖 **OS Map:**   OL 13

🖼 **Category:**   Current County Top, Marilyn

Coity Mountain (Mynydd Coety) stands at 1,896 ft (578 m). The flat-topped mountain falls on the border of both Torfaen and Blaenau Gwent counties so they share the same summit as their highest point.

Numerous rights-of-way cross over the mountain, although not over the summit. Most of the land is accessible and can be freely traversed on foot. Much of the mountain lies on the Blaenavon Industrial Landscape where a labyrinth of coal mines, including the Big Pit National Coal Museum, lay beneath the mountain.

LOG

Date:	**Week No:**
Start Point:	**Day:**
Start Time:	**Pace:**
Finish Time:	**Total Ascent:**
Elapsed Time:	**Total Distance:**

MYNYDD LLANGEINWYR

⛰ **Height:** 1,864 ft (568 m) ⊕ **County:** Bridgend

○ **Region:** Bridgend ◉ **Lat/Long:** 51.6412, -3.5726273

⊚ **Grid Ref:** SS 912 947 ▥ **OS Map:** OS 166

🖼 **Category:** Current County Top

Mynydd Llangeinwyr is the highest point in the county of Bridgend. It stands at 1,864 ft (568 m) and is situated in the South Wales Coalfield, a large region rich in coal deposits.

Numerous footpaths lead onto the hill from the surrounding communities and much of the land is open-access, allowing for the public to walk freely. A public bridleway also runs southwest from the A4107 across the summit.

LOG

Date:	**Week No:**
Start Point:	**Day:**
Start Time:	**Pace:**
Finish Time:	**Total Ascent:**
Elapsed Time:	**Total Distance:**

MOEL FAMAU

⛰ **Height:** 1,821 ft (555 m)   ⊕ **County:** Flintshire

○ **Region:** Clwydian Range   ◉ **Lat/Long:** 53.154, -3.25536349

◎ **Grid Ref:** SJ 161 626   🗺 **OS Map:** OS 265

🖼 **Category:** Historic County Top, Current County Top, Marilyn

Moel Famau stands at 1,821 ft (555 m) and is the highest point in the county of Flintshire. It is located within the Clwydian Range, a series of hills that run from Llandegla to Prestatyn. The hill is classed as an Area of Outstanding Natural Beauty and is surrounded by several Iron Age hillforts.

Numerous footpaths can be used to reach the summit, all with varying difficulties. Two of the more popular routes can be made from the car park between Moel Famau and Foel Fenlli. The Jubilee Tower sits at the summit. Although never completed due to a lack of funds, officials initially ordered the construction of the tower to commemorate the golden jubilee of George III in 1810.

LOG

Date:	Week No:
Start Point:	Day:
Start Time:	Pace:
Finish Time:	Total Ascent:
Elapsed Time:	Total Distance:

FOEL CWMCERWYN

Height: 1,759 ft (536 m) **County:** Pembrokeshire

Region: Pantmaenog Forest **Lat/Long:** 51.9461, -4.77472487

Grid Ref: SN 093 311 **OS Map:** OL 35

Category: Historic County Top, Current County Top, Marilyn

Foel Cwmcerwyn stands at 1,759 ft (536 m) high and is the highest point in the county of Pembrokeshire. It sits inside the Pembrokeshire Coast National Park. Officials established this park in 1952 because of its spectacular coastline of rugged cliffs and sandy beaches.

The hilltop sits roughly 10 km from the coast, above the small village of Rosebush, along the B4313. Here, a path to the summit can be found. A trig point is situated at the top of the hill and a number of cairns are scattered around the summit area.

LOG

Date:	Week No:
Start Point:	Day:
Start Time:	Pace:
Finish Time:	Total Ascent:
Elapsed Time:	Total Distance:

PEN MARCH & MERTHYR COMMON 16 & 17

△	**Height:** 1,755 ft (535 m)	⊕	**County:** Caerphilly / Merthyr Tydfil
○	**Region:** Brecon Beacons	◉	**Lat/Long:** 51.7333, -3.33824158
◉	**Grid Ref:** SO 082 110	▥	**OS Map:** OL 12
▣	**Category:** Current County Top		

At 1,755 ft (535 m) high, Pen March is joined with Merthyr Common, located a short distance away, whose highet is 1,742ft (531m). They are both located at the south-eastern part of the Brecon Beacons. Although the highest point of Merthyr common is located in the Merthyr Tydfil council area, Pen March falls within the county of Caerphilly.

An easy route to the summit, taking in both Merthyr Common and Pen March, can be made from Pontsticill Dam where tracks lead up around the north-western side of the hill. Pen March sits approximately 0.4 miles south of Merthyr Common.

LOG

Date:	**Week No:**
Start Point:	**Day:**
Start Time:	**Pace:**
Finish Time:	**Total Ascent:**
Elapsed Time:	**Total Distance:**

MYNYDD Y BETWS

⌂ **Height:** 1,224 ft (373 m)   ⊕ **County:** Swansea

○ **Region:** Swansea   ◉ **Lat/Long:** 51.767751, -3.936791

⊙ **Grid Ref:** SS 664 093   ▥ **OS Map:** OS 166

▨ **Category:** Current County Top, Marilyn

Mynydd y Betws has an elevation of 1,227 ft (374 m). It is a large hill in the city, and county, of Swansea. The hilltop is an area of upland with large stretches of grassland. The site is part of a wind farm with turbines towering up to 229 ft (70 m high). You can access the summit via a short walk from a small road that leads from Ammanford and Clydach.

Close to the top, you can also find the historic ruins of Penlle'r Castell, a medieval castle that is believed to date from around the late thirteenth century. Today, all that remains are a series of earthworks, deep ditches, and fragments of stones from the building that once stood there.

LOG

Date:	Week No:
Start Point:	Day:
Start Time:	Pace:
Finish Time:	Total Ascent:
Elapsed Time:	Total Distance:

WENTWOOD

⛰ **Height:** 1014 ft (309 m)   ⊕ **County:** Newport

◯ **Region:** Wentwood   ◉ **Lat/Long:** 51.6398, -2.85543793

◎ **Grid Ref:** ST 411 942   ▥ **OS Map:** OL 14

🖼 **Category:** Current County Top, Marilyn

Wentwood (Coed Gwent), at 1014 ft (309 m) high, is the highest point in the boundary of Newport. Parking can be found less than 500 m away from the summit. Views from the top provide a breath-taking overview of the River Severn Estuary.

This area is also home to the largest ancient woodland in Wales, with some trees dating back more than 400 years. It is also the ninth largest forest in the UK. Evidence of human existence dating back to prehistoric times can be found on Grey Hill in the form of burial mounds, a stone circle, and a megalithic alignment.

In the middle ages, the area was owned by the lordship of Chepstow. It acted as a hunting preserve and timber and fuel for local manors. Today, the area is popular with both hillwalkers and mountain bikers.

LOG

Date:	Week No:
Start Point:	Day:
Start Time:	Pace:
Finish Time:	Total Ascent:
Elapsed Time:	Total Distance:

△ **Height:** 1007 ft (307 m)   ⊕ **County:** Cardiff

○ **Region:** Cardiff   ⊙ **Lat/Long:** 51.543242, -3.2948749

⊙ **Grid Ref:** ST 103 835   🗺 **OS Map:** OS 151

🖼 **Category:** Current County Top, Marilyn

Garth Hill (Mynydd y Garth), at 1007 ft (307 m), is the highest point in Cardiff, located near the village of Pentyrch. The summit has a number of burial sites on its peak and can be reached from the village of Taff's Well. From here, it follows the Taff Ridgeway Walk to reach the top. The summit provides views across the city of Cardiff, the Taff Valley, and over the Bristol Channel. On clear sunny days, you can make out Weston-Super-Mare.

The hill is believed to be the inspiration behind the novel 'The Englishman who Went up a Hill but Came Down a Mountain' written by Christopher Monger.

LOG

Date:	**Week No:**
Start Point:	**Day:**
Start Time:	**Pace:**
Finish Time:	**Total Ascent:**
Elapsed Time:	**Total Distance:**

HOLYHEAD MOUNTAIN

⛰ **Height:** 720 ft (220 m)

⊕ **County:** Isle of Anglesey

◯ **Region:** Holy Island

◉ **Lat/Long:** 53.3134, -4.67560266

◉ **Grid Ref:** SH 218 829

▥ **OS Map:** OS 262

🖼 **Category:** Historic County Top, Current County Top, Marilyn

Standing at 720 ft (220 m), Holyhead mountain (Mynydd Twr) is the highest peak in the county of Anglesey. It is situated on Holy Island and protrudes into the Irish Sea. The eastern side of the mountain is the site of a late Roman watch tower called Carer y Twr, from which the Welsh name of the mountain is derived. South Stack Lighthouse is also located nearby.

The area attracts numerous visitors each year. Many people come to see the wide variety of nesting birds, including Atlantic Puffins, Stonechats, and Oyster Catchers. Extensive views are provided across to Ireland - the Wicklow mountains, the largest upland area in Ireland, can be seen on a clear day.

LOG

Date:	**Week No:**
Start Point:	**Day:**
Start Time:	**Pace:**
Finish Time:	**Total Ascent:**
Elapsed Time:	**Total Distance:**

TAIR ONNEN (PANTYLLADRON)

- ⌂ **Height:** 449 ft (137 m)
- ○ **Region:** Vale of Glamorgan
- ◉ **Grid Ref:** ST 036 739
- ⌷ **Category:** Current County Top
- ⊕ **County:** Vale of Glamorgan
- ◉ **Lat/Long:** 51.456609, -3.3879502
- ⌷ **OS Map:** OS 151

Tair Onnen (Pantylladron) is the smallest hill summit in Wales. Located in the county of Vale of Glamorgan, it stands at 449 ft (137 m) high and is located a short distance south of the A48, between the market town of Cowbridge (to the west) and the village of Bonvilston (to the East).

Access to the summit and trig point can easily be made from the A48. A public footpath runs along the edge of a solar farm.

LOG

Date:	Week No:
Start Point:	Day:
Start Time:	Pace:
Finish Time:	Total Ascent:
Elapsed Time:	Total Distance:

NORTHERN IRELAND COUNTY TOPS

Northern Ireland has the least number of counties, consisting of six unitary authorities. The table is listed in order from the highest county top to lowest.

☑

1.	Down	☐	2.	Derry	☐
3.	Tyrone	☐	4.	Fermanagh	☐
5.	Armagh	☐	6.	Antrim	☐

SLIEVE DONARD

⌂ **Height:** 2,790 ft (850 m) ⊕ **County:** Down

○ **Region:** Mourne Mountains⊕ **Lat/Long:** 54.179462, -5.922364

⊙ **Grid Ref:** J357 277 ▥ **OSNI Map:** Discoverer Series 29

▣ **Category:** Country High Point, Historic County Top, Current County Top, Marilyn, Hewitt, Vandeleur-Lynam

Slieve Donard (Sliabh Dónairt), standing at 2,790 ft (850 m), is the highest point in County Down, and the highest mountain in Northern Ireland. The mountain is situated in the Mourne Mountains, a granite mountain range. This area was proposed as the first national park in Northern Ireland.

The climb to the summit is fairly easy. The most popular way to reach it starts at Slieve Donard Forest on the north side of the mountain. A small tower, along with ancient prehistoric burial cairns, sits on the summit. One of these even appears to be a Neolithic passage tomb, the highest in both Britain and Ireland.

LOG

Date:		**Week No:**
Start Point:		**Day:**
Start Time:		**Pace:**
Finish Time:		**Total Ascent:**
Elapsed Time:		**Total Distance:**

SAWEL MOUNTAIN

⛰ **Height:** 2,224 ft (678 m)   🌐 **County:** Londonderry / Tyrone

⊙ **Region:** Sperrin Mountains   ◈ **Lat/Long:** 54.819715, -7.039362

◉ **Grid Ref:** H618 973   🗺 **OSNI Map:** Discoverer Series 13

🖼 **Category:** Historic County Top, Current County Top, Marilyn, Hewitt, Vandeleur-Lynam

Sawel Mountain (Samhail Phite Méabha), at 2,224 ft (678 m), is the highest point in both Londonderry and Tyrone. It is also the highest mountain in the Sperrin Mountains, one of the largest upland areas in Ireland spanning over 40 miles. Water on the hill is also the source of the River Faughan, a 29-mile long river that flows into the River Foyle.

The summit, composed of crystalline limestone, can be reached from Sperrin Road. A fence line leads all the way to the summit. A trig point can be found at the top to mark the summit itself.

LOG

Date:		**Week No:**	
Start Point:		**Day:**	
Start Time:		**Pace:**	
Finish Time:		**Total Ascent:**	
Elapsed Time:		**Total Distance:**	

CUILCAGH

◿	**Height:**	2,185 ft (666 m)	⊕ **County:**	Fermanagh
○	**Region:**	Breifne Mountains	⊙ **Lat/Long:**	54.200834, -7.812274
⊚	**Grid Ref:**	H123 281	▥ **OSNI Map:**	Discoverer Series 26
🖼	**Category:**	Historic County Top, Current County Top, Vandeleur-Lynam		

Culicagh (Binn Chuilceach), standing at 2,185 ft (666 m), sits on the Northern Ireland and Ireland border. It is the highest point in County Fermanagh. It is also the highest point of the Breifne Mountains, a range of hills stretching across three counties (Cavan, Fermanagh and Leitrim). It also sits on the border between Ireland and the United Kingdom.

The summit can be reached from the Cuilcagh mountain car park on Marlbank Road. From here, the route passes over and through one of the largest expanses of blanket bog in Northern Ireland, along farm tracks, boardwalks, and mountain paths before steeply climbing to reach the top.

LOG

Date:	**Week No:**
Start Point:	**Day:**
Start Time:	**Pace:**
Finish Time:	**Total Ascent:**
Elapsed Time:	**Total Distance:**

SLIEVE GULLION

- ⛰ **Height:** 1,880 ft (573 m)
- 🌐 **County:** Armagh
- ⊙ **Region:** Cooley Mountains
- ◉ **Lat/Long:** 54.119826, -6.434685
- ⊙ **Grid Ref:** J025 203
- 🗺 **OSNI Map:** Discoverer Series 29
- 🖼 **Category:** Historic County Top, Current County Top

Slieve Gullion (Sliabh gCuillinn), standing at, 1,880 ft (573 m), is the highest point in County Armagh. It is located in the heart of the Ring of Gullion, a geological formation and designated Area of Outstanding Natural Beauty.

The summit can be reached from a small car park halfway up the western side. A waymarked trail leads to the top. At the summit, you can find a small lake and two large ancient burial cairns, one of which is the highest surviving passage tomb in Ireland. The chamber inside measures 3.6 m wide and 4.3 m high. On a clear day, views from the summit extend as far away as Antrim, Dublin Bay, and Wicklow.

LOG

Date:	Week No:
Start Point:	Day:
Start Time:	Pace:
Finish Time:	Total Ascent:
Elapsed Time:	Total Distance:

TROSTAN

⛰ **Height:** 1,808 ft (551 m)   🌐 **County:** Antrim

⭘ **Region:** Antrim Hills   ◉ **Lat/Long:** 55.05, -6.166667

⊙ **Grid Ref:** D179 236   📖 **OSNI Map:** Discoverer Series 5

🖼 **Category:** Historic County Top, Current County Top, Marilyn

Trostan (Trostán), standing at 1,808 ft (551 m), is the highest point in County Antrim. The hill forms part of the Antrim Hills, a scenic expanse of exposed hills that are mostly covered in heather and tussock grasses.

The summit can be reached from Ballyeamon Road located to the east of the mountain. The Moyle Way, a long-distance path that explores a mixture of forest tracks and remote upland moor, also passes the slopes of Trostan. A trig point can be found marking the summit.

LOG

Date:	Week No:
Start Point:	Day:
Start Time:	Pace:
Finish Time:	Total Ascent:
Elapsed Time:	Total Distance:

NOTES

NOTES

Printed in Great Britain
by Amazon